How to Use an Interactive Whiteboard Really Effectively in Your Primary Classroom

Also available:

How to Use an Interactive Whiteboard Really Effectively in Your Secondary Classroom, Jenny Gage (ISBN 1-84312-262-6)

ICT for Teaching Assistants, John Galloway (ISBN 1-84312-203-0)

Learning on the Net, Alan Pritchard (ISBN 1-84312-082-8)

Help! There's a Computer in my Classroom, Alison Ball (ISBN 1-84312-119-0)

Creative ICT, Anthony Smith and Simon Willcox (ISBN 1-84312-136-0)

ICT in Primary Schools, 2nd Edition, Richard Ager (ISBN 1-84312-042-9)

Teaching the National Key Stage 3 Strategy, Clare Furlonger and Susan Haywood (ISBN 1-84312-029-1)

How to Use an Interactive Whiteboard Really Effectively in Your Primary Classroom

Jenny Gage

David Fulton Publishers

This edition reprinted 2008 by Routledge
2 Park Square, Milton Park, Abingdon, Oxon, OX14 4RN
Simultaneously published in the USA and Canada
By Routledge
270 Madison Avenue, New York, NY 10016

First published in Great Britain in 2005 by David Fulton Publishers
Reprinted 2006

10 9 8 7 6 5 4 3

British Library Cataloguing in Publication Data
A catalogue record for this book is available from the British Library.

ISBN 1 84312 235 9

Typeset by Servis Filmsetting Ltd, Manchester
Printed and bound in India by Replika Press Pvt. Ltd.

Contents

About the author

Jenny Gage has worked for the Millennium Mathematics Project (www.mmp. maths.org) since 2001. Based in the Mathematics and Education Faculties of the University of Cambridge, the MMP works to help people see how exciting maths can be, and to provide a range of projects to help them enjoy maths. Jenny's role is to organise the Motivate videoconferencing project (www.motivate.maths.org), which provides videoconferences and accompanying project work for school students of all ages on a variety of mathematical and scientific topics. She also develops mathematical resources for the interactive whiteboard and gives courses for teachers on using an interactive whiteboard in the maths lesson.

Before working for the MMP, Jenny was a teacher for 15 years, teaching maths in schools in Derbyshire, Milton Keynes and Buckinghamshire. She also worked for the Open University for 15 years as a tutor on a number of maths courses. From 1998 until 2004, she carried out research for her PhD on how graphic calculators could help children in the 10–14 year age range to learn the basics of algebra.

When she isn't working, Jenny enjoys playing the piano, choral singing and going to concerts, and she always has at least one book on the go, often a thriller or a travel book. There is always time to read! She also enjoys exploring new places, both in the UK and abroad. Jenny is married with four grown-up children and two cats.

To Robert, Helen, James and Heather

who helped me in all sorts of ways, and who are representative of the children
whose learning will be enhanced by the interactive whiteboard

Acknowledgements

I am very grateful to the Headteachers of Harston and Newton Primary School and Foxton Primary School, Cambridgeshire for permission to observe and take photographs during lessons that involved use of the interactive whiteboard in their schools, and to interview staff and pupils. Names of pupils have been changed to protect their anonymity. I would particularly like to thank Jemma Griffith and Jane Dicker, whose help has been invaluable.

I am grateful to Oxfam for permission to use a poster from their range of educational material; to Graham Colman of Taverham School, Norfolk for permission to use a photograph of the Transit of Venus; and to the Dean and Chapter of Ely Cathedral for permission to take and use photographs in the cathedral. Images used in *The_Solar_System.ppt*, which is on the accompanying CD and described in Chapter 9, are courtesy NASA/JPL-Caltech.

I would also like to thank Margaret Allen of Promethean Ltd and Jon Sugden of Smarter-Solutions Ltd for checking the detailed sections on ACTIVprimary and SMARTboard software. Needless to say, any errors that remain are my own.

I would like to acknowledge the help of my nieces and nephew Heather, Helen and James in commenting on their experiences with the interactive whiteboard, and providing me with raw material for some of the resources in this book.

Finally, I want to thank my husband Andrew, whose suggestions and proofreading were a great help, and whose cooking and shopping helped me to complete this book more or less on time.

Introduction

'I wouldn't be without them. All my teachers have them. I think they are one of the most important tools around for teachers right now.'

'I've got one, but I only use it with the data projector for showing PowerPoint or videos. I can't see what all the fuss is about.'

'We're supposed to be getting them soon, but it seems to me that it's an awful lot of money to spend. It will take so much longer to prepare lessons if we've got to find out how to do everything differently.'

Interactive whiteboards (IWBs) are rapidly entering our classrooms, for some bringing excitement or anxiety, but leaving others wondering what all the fuss is about. While I was writing this book, I visited a number of primary schools, finding out how they were using interactive whiteboards in the classroom, and about teachers' attitudes to them. The comments above indicate something of the range of opinion I found.

Some teachers are excited by this new piece of technology. They look forward to finding out what they can do with it, and how it can be used to enhance their teaching. Even experienced users say they have yet to use anything like the full potential of the board. Others wonder if they will ever get the hang of using it, fearing it will let them down at a crucial moment. There are also those who feel that it has nothing to offer that they cannot achieve in other ways.

Of course, no piece of equipment, however wonderful, can make anyone a better teacher by itself. An IWB is a tool which, when used well, will help a teacher to teach well. However, a poor lesson will remain exactly that if the IWB is used in a way that is unsuitable and irrelevant. In the hands of a good teacher, an IWB can make lessons exciting, interactive and well-paced, motivating the children, and providing them with experiences they remember. An IWB can be used to support good lessons, full of interest, with well-thought out content and authentic tasks. Equally, it can be used to support inappropriate lesson content and style, providing an excuse for tedious, one-way lessons that are only remembered because they are so boring.

Although an IWB is called 'interactive', interaction is not really about the board. Interaction should be between the children, the teacher and the subject content of the lesson. It is not the board which determines how much interaction occurs, but the teacher using it. Effective use of an IWB should encourage both teachers and children to ask deeper, more probing questions, and to search for answers together. An IWB can provide a focus for children to contribute their ideas, and to listen to those of others. It can also lead to greater incorporation of ICT, so that ICT is integrated into the curriculum, rather than seen as a separate subject, only met in the ICT suite.

The purpose of this book is to help teachers to use an IWB in a way that supports effective practice and enhances learning. It is intended both for teachers who have little or no experience of using an IWB, and for those who feel that they have mastered one aspect of the board's use, but would like to find out more about what it can do to support their teaching. It is not meant to present a complete range of resources; many resources can now be found on the internet, and some suggestions are given at the end of the book for such websites. What I hope the resources in this book will do is to help teachers to explore what they can do with their interactive whiteboards, so that, having tried out these particular resources and the techniques they contain, they can then move on to prepare their own resources.

Detailed instructions are given for the use of commonly available software such as Microsoft Word, Excel and Paint, and presentation software, such as Microsoft PowerPoint and the software that comes with the IWB. There are a number of makes of board available, and it has not been possible to provide specific instructions for all these. I have decided to focus on the SMARTboard and Promethean's ACTIVprimary software. Using SMARTboard software is very similar to using Microsoft products, and SMARTboards are to be found in many primary schools, so this was an obvious choice. Using ACTIVprimary software is rather different, but the ACTIVprimary system contains such a vast wealth of material for use in primary schools, that again it seemed an obvious choice. I hope that teachers with other boards will nevertheless find much that is helpful to them, and that, with their own Users Guide to help, they will be able to make use of the suggestions in this book.

The book is accompanied by a CD, containing all the resources described in this book. These are available for teachers to use and edit as they wish. Resources are in Microsoft Word, Excel and PowerPoint (XP versions, 2003), SMARTboard notebooks (version 8.1.2, 2004) and ACTIVprimary flipcharts (version 1.1.23, 2004). Microsoft resources should open in other versions of the software. If you do not have the most up-to-date version of the SMARTboard or ACTIVprimary software, these can usually be downloaded from their websites, or bought for a small additional payment. (See the Appendix for website addresses.) Promethean are bringing out a new version of ACTIVprimary software later in 2004, which will improve it further.

This book is divided into three parts. Part 1, The Interactive Whiteboard in the Classroom, covers practical and pedagogical issues. In Chapter 1, basic practical matters are considered, such as what can the IWB do, what types are there, and where should it be put. The question of how an IWB can enhance teaching and learning in the primary school teaching is discussed in Chapter 2. Does it take up a lot of time to prepare materials for it? Does it help integrate ICT into the curriculum? In Chapter 3, the pedagogy of teaching with an IWB is discussed. How is an IWB best used in the classroom? How does its use affect teaching and learning? Is it only for use with the whole class? How does its use affect different types of learners? What about children with special educational needs?

Part 2, Getting Started, covers technical matters. In Chapter 4, the functionality of an IWB is described, together with suggestions for getting started. A good way to get started is with a favourite piece of software or website, used with the IWB's annotation tools. In Chapter 5, instructions are given for common operations in various different applications, such as printing and saving, creating templates, and using presentation software. Applications covered include Microsoft Word, PowerPoint, Excel and Paint and IWB software. Chapter 6 then gives a detailed overview of ACTIVprimary software and SMARTboard software, with descriptions of what the various menus and tools do. These are also tabulated for easy reference in Appendices 2 and 3.

In Part 3, Lesson Resources, there are many detailed ideas for using the IWB in the curriculum. Most of the resources given, which are available on the accompanying CD, relate to the English and Mathematics areas of the curriculum, but others are relevant to topics in Geography, History, Science, Personal, Social and Health Education and the Citizenship curricular areas. Several of the resources are cross-curricular.

It is hoped that teachers will perhaps start by using the resources provided on the CD, then edit these to suit their own practice, and finally move on to use the techniques and ideas they have gained to make their own resources. The ideas discussed in this section are meant to be a starting point, enabling teachers to create their own lesson materials, not a static set of resources. Full details are given to help teachers edit the files provided on the CD, and to personalise them for use in their own classrooms. Many of the ideas, although put in the context of a particular resource, could be applied to many other topic areas. For simplicity, I have used 'she' to refer to the primary class teacher.

It is my belief that the interactive whiteboard has the ability to transform our classrooms, bringing action, colour and variety to teaching and learning. All the children I spoke to were very enthusiastic about its impact on their lessons and the teachers who were already using the IWB were excited by the possibilities. I hope that this book will help others to explore for themselves the potential of the interactive whiteboard.

Interactive Whiteboard CD-ROM

Minimum requirements to run the CD-ROM:
- PC only
- 700 MHz
- 64 Mb RAM
- CD-ROM
- Windows 98 SE, 2000, XP Home or Pro (SP1)
- Mouse or pointing device

In addition you will need Microsoft Office 2000 (or better). Smartboard or ACTIVprimary software to actually use the templates included.

If your CD does not start automatically after a few seconds, explore the CD and open the file "START.EXE".

Users who have the software Macromedia Flash MX studio or other Macromedia Flash authoring software may experience difficulty in opening ACTIVprimary work files when they click on the activity buttons of the CD-ROM. In some cases, the Macromedia software may attempt to (incorrectly) open the files.

This difficulty is due to both types of software using the same file extension (.FLP).

As a workaround the user may either:
- Uninstall the Macromedia Flash software
- Open the ACTIVprimary software and locate the following folders on the CD-ROM:
      MATHS_RESOURCES
      ENGLISH_RESOURCES
      OTHER_RESOURCES

The files can then be opened from within the ACTIVprimary software.

PART 1

The Interactive Whiteboard in the Classroom

First, what is an interactive whiteboard? It is essentially a large computer screen, which is sensitive to touch. To operate an IWB, there needs to be a computer and a data projector in addition to the board itself. The content of the computer screen is displayed on the board using the data projector, and the computer can then be operated either from the computer mouse and keyboard, or directly from the whiteboard. With some boards, a finger can be used to write and draw on them and to operate software; other boards require special pens (which are equivalent to the mouse on a conventional computer).

An IWB can be used to replace the ordinary whiteboard and the overhead projector. In addition, it can be used to demonstrate and annotate web resources or any computer application or file on the school computer network. IWBs can also be used with video, music and picture files. If there is a scanner available, or if children are working at networked computers, then their work can be displayed to the rest of the class on the IWB, and saved as a record of their progress. In fact, anything displayed on the board, including annotations, can be saved for later, and/or printed.

The IWB is an excellent way of incorporating greater use of ICT in a way that does not lead to a teacher feeling redundant, exhausted or deskilled. The role of the teacher is central to effective practice in the use of ICT in the classroom, but unfortunately all too often ICT use can make a teacher feel that the children know more than she does, and that her role is to rush round fielding technical problems. With an IWB, the teacher remains in control of what happens and what is discussed, so that important educational points can be focused on, rather than lost in the technicalities.

IWB use can support the use of other ICT in the classroom, by:

- providing access to a wide range of computer software and programs without the need to go to a computer suite

- providing a focus for the children's attention

- providing a large display

- encouraging discussion about issues other than technical problems.

New ICT applications can be demonstrated by the teacher first, so that the children can see what is expected of them, and what they should achieve. Teachers can intervene as they see fit: if the children are working at individual computers, they can be stopped to focus on the IWB at points where discussion between the whole class and the teacher would be beneficial.

However, IWB use is not simply about incorporating more ICT in lessons. As we shall see, the IWB can provide a dynamic approach to teaching and learning resources that has the potential to revolutionise our classrooms.

CHAPTER 1

Practical matters

What is an interactive whiteboard?

An IWB can be thought of as a mix of a computer, an overhead projector and a whiteboard (or chalkboard).

The interactive whiteboard as a computer

An interactive whiteboard is run by a computer, and the whiteboard display is exactly the same as the display on the computer monitor. The board acts as an extra computer screen, but with the additional property of being interactive. Some interactive whiteboards have special pens which act like a computer mouse, with other types a finger can be used (although a wet finger will not work). Boards that can be operated directly with a finger may also have special pens.

Any software or files that are available on the computer can be accessed using the pen/finger and used on the IWB. This can be done either through the computer keyboard, or directly on the board by clicking or tapping with the pen/finger. The board will probably also have an onscreen keyboard, so that text can be typed directly without having to use the computer keyboard. The onscreen keyboard is operated by tapping on the keys required.

An IWB also allows interactive use of the internet. To do this, open up an internet connection on the computer and a suitable site. Then use the pen/finger to work directly on the board, rather than working from the computer keyboard. This is particularly useful for displaying and working with a site with a whole class: the site can be clearly seen by all the children at the same time so that they are all focused on the same thing.

The interactive whiteboard as an overhead projector

Teachers who have used OHPs in the past will have banks of transparencies that they will want to be able to continue to use. Provided there is a scanner available, any worksheet or transparency can be scanned into the computer, so that it is then accessible on the IWB.

The IWB has annotation tools which allow a document to be written on, highlighted, and drawn on: the document can be annotated in the same way as an OHP transparency. The contents of the document can also be revealed bit by bit, as with an OHP. Most IWB software has a tool which puts a black screen over the document, which can then be pulled back gradually.

The advantage the IWB has over an ordinary OHP is that everything can be saved for another time, including both original documents and annotated documents. Either can also be printed if desired. Unlike overhead transparencies, these files will not be lost or become messy. They are always there, on the computer system, as good as new.

The interactive whiteboard as a whiteboard/chalkboard

As its name suggests, an IWB is also a whiteboard or chalkboard. Whereas using the IWB as a computer or overhead projector really only requires a data projector and computer, apart from the use of the special annotation tools, using the IWB as a whiteboard involves opening up the IWB software. On a SMARTboard, this is called a notebook; in ACTIVprimary, it is known as a flipchart.

The IWB notebook or flipchart has far more clean pages ready for use than anyone is ever likely to use in a lesson. One click or tap on the appropriate icon will bring up a clean page whenever it is needed. However, the previous pages will still be available, so they can be returned to if required. All the pages used can be displayed to allow easy navigation between them, or so that their order can be changed.

Unlike a conventional whiteboard, a variety of colours is available for the background colour. A white background can cause glare, preventing some children from seeing properly; this can be avoided if a different colour is chosen. Many other backgrounds are usually also available, including square grids and lines for handwriting.

Different types of IWBs

There are two main types of IWB available. One type has a sensitive board surface, which may mean you can use your finger to write on the board, or to change from one program to another. This is especially useful for younger children, who find pen control difficult. They can write or draw directly on the board, without needing to worry about using a pen. A well-known make of board with a sensitive surface, which can be operated using just fingers, is the SMARTboard. SMARTboards also have a tray containing pens, which write like ordinary whiteboard pens (although they do not use real ink!). In addition, the SMARTboard website has lesson plans, case studies and downloadable classroom resources, although not all are particularly appropriate for the UK curriculum. This type of board is proving to be very popular with many schools, particularly in the primary sector.

The second main type of IWB has a surface which is not touch-sensitive, and needs a special mouse pen. The electronics are inside the board, which makes this type of board less likely to be damaged, since their surfaces can take a reasonable degree of normal wear and tear. Well-known makes include the Promethean ACTIVboards and the Hitachi board. The Promethean ACTIVboard is the most expensive board, but has the most complete software. Promethean sell complete educational systems including software, and their Activ Primary is specially made for primary education. Their boards and software have been specifically designed with an educational focus. The Promethean website has a wide range of classroom resources, lesson plans, case studies, user groups, training and conference details.

Some types of board also provide slates or tablets which can be used by children at their own tables or anywhere else in the room. Another facility offered by some manufacturers is a 'voting system'. Each child has a hand-held voting keypad which uses radio communication. The teacher puts a question up on the board, with various choices for the answer. Each child's choice is then recorded, so that a record can be kept of both class performance on the questions and each child's individual performance.

Cables for equipment connected with wires need to be dealt with safely. They can be largely eliminated by using wireless boards, projectors, tablets, slates, keyboards, and so on. As well as contributing to the overall safety of the classroom, these also mean that teachers can walk about as they wish, instead of being pinned at the front of the room next to the IWB. Children can also display their work, without having to move about the classroom.

Fixed or mobile?

Most makes of board give the option of having them fixed to the wall or free-mounted on their own stand. Both have advantages and disadvantages. A wall-mounted board is less vulnerable to damage, or to movement during a lesson, which could mean it needs recalibrating. However, once a board is mounted on the wall and the data projector on the ceiling, it is more or less permanently fixed. A board on a wheeled stand together with an unmounted data projector can be used anywhere around the school, which provides much greater flexibility of use.

The needs of all the children and the teacher should be considered in deciding whether to go for fixed boards or not. It is important that every child has a clear view of the board, and can easily reach the board to use it. If the room does not have blinds, the board needs to be sited so that it is not in direct sunlight, as this will mean that it is difficult to see anything except the glare of reflected light. An adequate data projector is also important if children are to see what is on the board clearly. Whether the board is fixed or mobile, make sure there is enough room around the board to stand without casting a shadow on the board. Children learn quite quickly to stand to one side or kneel down to avoid this.

The height of the board is also an important consideration: the height that is comfortable for the teacher is probably too high for the children, and vice versa. Mobile boards can be put at different heights on the stand, but the lowest height may still be too high for smaller children. Children at the back of the room may also find it difficult to see what is at the bottom of a board mounted in a low position. A way round this problem is to use a step for smaller children to stand on.

The board needs to be easily accessible by all the children: if it takes more than a brief interval for a child to reach the board to contribute something, it is unlikely that this will happen very often. Access to the room and the board needs to be considered for children in wheelchairs or with mobility problems. One way to ensure access, if the room is big enough, is to have a space in front of the board, where the children can sit on the floor.

Experience seems to indicate that a fixed board in a teacher's own classroom will be used regularly and frequently. Access to the board is not a problem; the teacher has the opportunity to get used to using the board, and does not need to spend precious time setting up the board or the projector. On the other hand, if either the board or projector, or both, is not permanently set up, a good 15 minutes can be lost at the beginning of the day, or the lesson, getting this done. In these circumstances, teachers are much less likely to use the board on a regular basis, and so are less likely to become effective users.

There will need to be a PC or laptop sited near the board, and the positioning of this also needs careful consideration: both ease of use and safety need to be considered. To gain the full benefit of the IWB, the PC or laptop should be connected to the school computer network and to the internet. If it is networked, then work done by children at other computers can easily be displayed, and resources can be shared by all the staff. However, speed of logging onto the school network may be a problem for teachers not teaching in their own rooms. If the board is sited in the room the teacher is going to use all day, this is not an issue, because it can be turned on and any setting up done first thing in the morning, but it may be a problem for a teacher who walks into a different room, expecting to be able to get on with the lesson straight away.

Technical problems also need to be considered. Particularly when teachers lack experience with IWBs, any technical problems may mean that a planned lesson cannot proceed. This could be due to network failure or equipment failure, or simply to use by an inexperienced person. This is not to say that an inexperienced teacher is more likely to have things go wrong, but that they may have less idea of what to do to remedy a problem. Whatever the cause, teachers need to have an alternative strategy they can use if the board refuses to co-operate and cannot be speedily fixed. Often rebooting the computer, and restarting the software helps. If this does not sort out the problem, it is better to do something else than to keep everyone waiting longer.

Cheaper alternatives to an IWB

Some schools decide to start with just a data projector, rather than the more expensive IWB. This will display the computer screen onto any white surface, showing whatever is on the computer monitor. Resources can be prepared in advance, and saved for another occasion. If the image is projected onto an ordinary whiteboard, then it can be annotated, so that some of the advantages of the IWB are available. PowerPoint presentations can also be annotated using the mouse. However, the annotations cannot be saved as they could with an IWB, neither is the whiteboard surface interactive. This means all changes need to be made at the computer keyboard, and the dynamic qualities of an IWB are not available.

Another option might be to convert an ordinary whiteboard to an electronic board. These allow the movement of ordinary dry marker pens to be tracked using ultrasound, which is then converted to a computer file, so that the content of the board can be saved, printed out, and used again as desired. Although such systems are not actually IWBs, they allow anything written or drawn on an existing whiteboard to be captured, annotated and edited. These have the advantage of being light, portable and inexpensive as they can be used with existing conventional whiteboards.

CHAPTER 2

How can an interactive whiteboard enhance teaching and learning in the primary school?

There are many case studies describing some aspect of interactive whiteboard (IWB) use on the internet these days. These are some of the advantages suggested by its advocates:

- it helps teachers to structure their lessons

- it enables ICT use to be more integrated into lessons

- it helps to attract and retain children's attention

- it provides large attractive text and images

- text and images may be moved around the board and/or changed

- many boards have additional software which provides a variety of additional graphics, such as maps, specialist backgrounds, and a wide range of images

- it supports collaborative learning

- it can help develop children's cognitive skills

- it saves time taken up in note-taking or scribing

- work can be saved for later or printed out.

Some research has suggested that high IWB use leads to more questioning, both of children and by them, more stimulating discussion, and better explanations. Children enjoy the additional variety which IWB use allows. Many different resources can be used in a lesson, and these can be returned to whenever necessary. Moving frequently between resources helps children to refocus their attention if they were distracted, helping them to stay on task for longer.

Some children benefit from being able to touch the board, and physically move objects around it. Using audio and video files allows voices from outside the classroom to be heard, again refocusing attention. All learners can benefit from the increased opportunities for more auditory learning, more visual learning and more kinaesthetic learning.

Some who are unconvinced by the claims of the IWB suggest that using a data projector alone can give teachers all the additional functionality they need. With a data projector and a computer, a teacher has access to the internet and to any software application available in school. Others, who believe that the IWB offers significantly more than a data projector and computer, point to the fact that annotations can be saved and printed out, that images can be made dynamic, so that they can be moved across the page, changed in colour or size, or animated, and that text, graphics, video and sound can all be incorporated into presentations.

This need not be an either/or choice, however. Sometimes cost will dictate what equipment is available. Starting with a data projector and a computer in the classroom will enable teachers to start using more resources. If at some later point, an IWB can also be provided, these teachers will be well on the way to using it effectively. Many of the resources provided in this book, and its accompanying CD, can be used with just a data projector and computer. The difference an IWB offers is the software that comes with it, and this is where the truly dynamic resources can be made.

Access

Access to an IWB on a regular basis is crucial, if teachers are to integrate it into their lessons. If teachers do not have reliable access to a board, it is very unlikely that they will move beyond using the board in a very basic way. There is also a risk that the board is used 'because it's my turn', rather than because it is an effective and appropriate means of delivering the planned lesson. If a school only has one or two boards, teachers need to be sure that if they spend time preparing a lesson using the IWB, it will actually be available on the day.

If teachers do not have regular access to a board, this may be because it is not in their usual teaching room. Going to another room, then starting up the computer and the board could waste valuable teaching time. If, however, a teacher has a board in her own room, all the equipment can be started up at the beginning of the day, before the children arrive, and any problems can be dealt with immediately. On the other hand, a class of restive children, waiting to get on with their work, will make any problems seem much worse, and could lead to the planned lesson being abandoned altogether.

Access to the IWB also involves knowing how to start it and how to open resources. One teacher I spoke to said she was quite keen to have a go, but had so far failed. The first time she tried to use the board, she could not work out how to get it going. The next time, she could not work out how to access any resources. Then a stack of library books was placed in front of the board, so preventing her from trying again. As a result she had decided to leave it until the summer holidays.

Training

It is quite possible to use an IWB like an ordinary whiteboard (although possibly using special pens) and never make any use of its functionality. This may happen if teachers do not currently use ICT much, and are given no training in the use of the IWB. But what an expensive whiteboard it then becomes! It is important that teachers have the time and help they need to become confident in their use of the IWB, so that they do not stick with just a few basic operations. Having said that, there will be occasions when use of the IWB is restricted to simply using it as a whiteboard, because that is what is appropriate. There is no reason why teachers should feel they have to do something innovative or creative with it every lesson.

The IWB screen is a Windows environment like any other computer likely to be found in a school, so teachers need to be familiar with Windows, and know how to access and manipulate the software and files on the system they have in school. Once teachers have a basic familiarity with Windows, and one or two types of software, then using the IWB should not be a problem. A teacher new to the IWB can start with a program they are already accustomed to using, allowing them to learn how to use the board with a familiar activity. There is a learning curve in finding out all that it can do, but there is no reason why this should not be a gradual learning curve, which teachers take at the pace that suits them. Those who are worried about their keyboard or mouse skills will find that these soon improve with practice.

Beyond the stage of computer familiarisation, more time and training will be needed if a teacher is to become an effective IWB user. Quite how much time this will take will depend to an extent on how much teachers already incorporate ICT into their lessons. Teachers who already use, say, a word processor, specialist software, or the internet with their classes will have a head start over those who use ICT very little.

Where teachers do not already use ICT very much, IWB familiarisation will initially add to preparation time, but this should decrease as they become accustomed to how the board functions. Sharing resources with colleagues helps to reduce preparation time, particularly once a bank of lesson ideas has been built up. If a novice can be paired with a more experienced user, this will also help, particularly if they can team teach with the IWB from time to time.

It is an advantage to teachers to have access to a laptop, so that they can take the IWB software home with them, providing opportunities to explore the board's capabilities and to prepare resources. An alternative might be to make the IWB software available to teachers to take home to install on home computers. Files can be brought into school on floppy disks or CDs, or sent as email attachments. Becoming proficient in using the IWB requires time and the opportunity for private exploration of what the board can do in an unpressurised atmosphere that allows teachers to think creatively.

To move beyond using familiar software only, teachers will need to become familiar with the general operation of their boards. This means knowing how to access and use the free-floating annotation tools (pens, highlighters, erasers and so on) that are provided by the board's own software. Figure 2.1 shows the annotation tools for the SMARTboard software (left-hand set of tools) and ACTIVprimary software (right-hand set of tools). These can be used to write notes on any application, including Word and PowerPoint, highlight text, draw arrows to particular items, and so on. These tools also contain a 'camera' tool, which can be used to make a copy of any part of the screen. Using these tools will be discussed in more detail in Chapter 4.

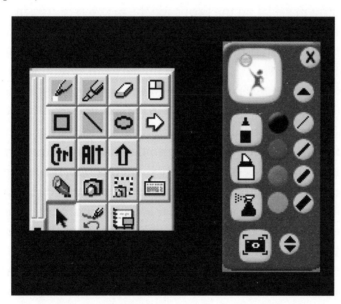

Figure 2.1 Floating annotation tools (SMARTboard tools on the left, ACTIVprimary tools on the right)

In addition to annotation tools, which can be used with any application or the internet, IWBs also have their own software which teachers can use to produce their own presentations.

Learning how to use an IWB effectively can be speeded up by training courses provided by the LEA or by independent trainers, or by getting someone from the company selling the board to come and demonstrate how the board works, and how to start using it. However, if teachers cannot follow up their training by using the board regularly, they will soon forget what they have been taught, and need to spend time going over the training again. Regardless of the training provided, time needs to be put aside for teachers to practise before using the board in front of the class, and for them to make classroom resources.

Lesson preparation

An aspect of good preparation is choosing the best tool for the job; this means not using an IWB just because it is there. There will be times when the IWB is not the best way to present a topic, and of course it will always be necessary for children to work with practical materials. No simulation can provide everything that using hands-on resources can.

Another factor to consider is whether a lesson needs a new approach. The lessons to start incorporating IWB use in are probably not those that are already very good. If you have a lesson which scores nine out of a possible ten, why mess around with it? However, if you have a lesson which you would only score at six out of ten, say, then that might be a good one to reconsider and to plan using the IWB.

It appears to be the experience of many teachers already using an IWB that any additional preparation means their lessons are better prepared. Such time is not necessarily lost to them, either. Instead of spending break or the lunch hour in the classroom putting material on the board for the next lesson, the teacher can have everything ready on the IWB beforehand. If a teacher wants to continue something begun earlier, she can just open up the file, and carry on – no need to write things up again.

In fact, the teachers I spoke to said they were not spending any more time on preparation than they always had. They also emphasised that they were thinking more about how a resource would help the children to learn, rather than simply what needed to be taught. One said: 'I spend the same amount of time, but I get a lot more out of it.' Another said she actually spent less time preparing, because she could pull things up from last week or last year if she wanted to, without starting from scratch. She also commented that her resources were far more professional looking. In addition, using the IWB helped her with planning ahead.

Using an IWB need not mean always starting from scratch on preparing new resources and ideas. Because anything on the IWB can be saved on the school network, resources can be shared between teachers. If a colleague has already prepared IWB resources for a particular lesson, these can be used as a starting point, or indeed, just used as they are. If teachers share what they do in this way, a bank of resources will soon accumulate, and over time will be worked on, and improved. Many LEAs already provide banks of resources on their websites, as does the Standards Site of the DfES.

Support for subject areas

IWB software has many resources and tools which can be used to support subject areas. These range from having calculator, protractor and ruler tools, to being able to access presentations on the Tudors or on magnets, say, or an animation of a compass. Images, such as coins, musical instruments, geographical features and scientific equipment are available to illustrate teaching resources. One teacher I interviewed commented on how much easier it was to do a topic on money with realistic coins to display.

Backgrounds available include square grids, handwriting lines and a variety of maps. Being able to use squared or graph paper and really straight lines means that graphs are correctly drawn, and children no longer have to use their imaginations to work out what they should look like. Some software also includes music and other sounds. Further resources can be downloaded from a wide range of websites, including the manufacturers' websites, the DfES Standards website, LEA websites, other schools, and many others (see Appendix 1 for further details).

Ownership

Material can be personalised, so that a class has ownership of it in a way that is not possible with books and worksheets. A particular example of this is given in Chapter 7, where details are given of how children can construct an audio book about themselves. A book can be produced that looks as if it were professionally produced, and can be printed out if desired. Such a book can include children's own drawings and handwriting, as well as word processed text, which can be printed out to form a record. Another example of personalisation could be the construction of a book to record a visit or activity. Photos or video could be incorporated together with text and a spoken narration.

In Chapter 9, a map activity is described that uses the annotation tools provided by the IWB. This could be made the occasion of developing an awareness of where towns in the UK and elsewhere are (using the maps of the UK, Europe or the world available with many types of IWB software). Perhaps children could bring in envelopes to school, and mark on the map where they originated. If material is worked on by a class, teacher and children together, then that class has ownership of it. This is no longer just a map of Britain with some towns on it. It is a map showing where Alice's auntie lives, where Hasan's father's electricity bill comes from, and so on.

Integrating ICT into lessons

Proponents of ICT use in the classroom claim many benefits for its use. These often include interactivity, provisionality, access to information, and the speeding up of routine tasks. Certainly, a great benefit of ICT for many children is its provisionality. If something is incorrect, there is no need to cross it out, it can simply be deleted, and something else substituted. This means that ideas can be tried out without loss of face. This is particularly helpful for children who find writing difficult.

We have access to more information today than ever before, and the amount of information 'out there' is growing all the time. It is therefore increasingly important that children learn how to use the internet safely and appropriately. They need to know how to evaluate what they read on the internet, and to realise that sites may not have accurate information. Tasks such as collecting and displaying data can now be done quickly and effectively with appropriate software, calculations can be carried out, and results displayed using presentation software. Time saved on these tasks can be used to help children develop higher-order thinking skills, such as deciding what are good questions to research or good keywords for a search, what aspects of data should be displayed and how this should be done.

Unfortunately, there have been occasions where teachers have interpreted their role when ICT is used as one of merely facilitating the children's interactions with the software and managing the classroom. Of course, these are important, but it is also necessary for the teacher to continue to support the children's learning by asking questions, probing to see how well they understand. The IWB can help this to occur, by providing a focus for the children. Where computers are networked, any one computer screen could be shown on the IWB screen, allowing the teacher to use this for making a teaching point.

In many lessons in which ICT is used, the ICT diverts attention from the subject issues to concerns with ICT skills. Rather than using ICT to enable them to understand a concept better, children worry about which key to press, how to rescue things when suddenly they have something different on their screen from everyone else, which font to use, and so on. The teachers' job rapidly becomes one of rushing round the room from one pair of children to another, unable to spend more than a few seconds with any one pair, if uproar is not to break out in the room generally.

In an atmosphere like this, there is no opportunity for teachers to monitor, scrutinise or evaluate what the children are doing. Work done may contain factual inaccuracies, be of questionable relevance to the topic under consideration, with more attention paid to the look of the work than to its content. Discussion between pairs of children at a computer is often about technical issues, rather than the subject matter, or arguments about whose turn it is to control the mouse. Printing out a piece of work becomes an end rather than an opportunity for evaluation and reflection.

Using an IWB makes it much easier to incorporate ICT into lessons, and to demonstrate new ICT skills. There are of course many occasions when children need to be working at their own computers, but equally there are other occasions when it makes better sense for all the children to be focused on the same computer screen so that there can be discussion among the class of issues other than how to operate the computer or which key to press. If a teacher is trying to teach children how to use a program, it is much more effective to do this with them all focused on one large screen, than rush round 15 different computers, saying the same thing over and over. IWBs also provide large versions of a keyboard (Figure 2.2) which can be shown onscreen, and used to demonstrate keyboard skills.

Figure 2.2 Onscreen keyboard

However, although an IWB makes demonstrating software much more straight-forward, it would be a pity to limit use of the IWB to this, since there is so much more that can be done with it. Data logging equipment can be used with an IWB in science lessons. Simulations help children to understand new concepts. Music software can make them into composers. Word processing software and spread-sheets provide opportunities in English and Maths. On the internet, children can be taught how to search for suitable websites, or can be shown different websites which they can then evaluate. The use of email can be demonstrated. Video and audio clips can be added to presentations. Digital cameras can be used to add pictures to a resource, or pictures and text scanned in from other sources. The sky really is the limit!

Professional presentation

Of necessity, the display on an ordinary whiteboard is static and impermanent, and can only consist of anything that can be drawn on it, written on it, or stuck to it. Additional resources used, such as laminated cards, often get lost or dog-eared. The IWB display, however, can be permanent, always available, and always in perfect condition. Such displays can be dynamic, and can call up a host of resources from the school network and the worldwide web. Teachers and children using an IWB can easily achieve a level of presentation that matches professionally designed resources, unlike much that is drawn or written on an ordinary board. Once teachers become used to using the IWB, resources which would have been printed on card and stuck to the board become a thing of the past.

This is particularly useful in areas of the curriculum where visual resources are important, such as Mathematics, Science, Geography and Art: 'In Art – if you are talking about a picture you could see it . . . and it means you can discuss it as a class' (Rachel, aged 11). With an IWB, a teacher can produce a map, correct in every detail, virtually instantaneously. The map can be written across, have places marked on it, special features drawn onto it, and be saved for another occasion.

The original is also available for another time, still in perfect condition. Video, diagrams and images which are large, clear, in colour and dynamic make it easier for children to understand complex concepts, and remember them. Video clips can be stopped at any point, annotated using the IWB floating tools, and then started again. In some types of IWB software, the image with its annotations can be saved, and made part of notes printed out for the children.

Creating records

The IWB could also be used to create and save records for each child in the class. Each child's record might contain an example of their handwriting, contributions they had made to class discussion, and examples of presentations they had made. On any particular occasion, a small group could add examples of their work to their file on the whiteboard. If this is then saved, there will be an exact, permanent record of their work, which can be compared over time, and used to facilitate report-writing. There is no need to keep lots of books or pieces of paper, just a file on the computer.

Using the IWB to support home-school links

Keeping parents up-to-date with how much their child's writing has improved, say, is easy: the child's work can be saved and printed out for them to take home. If the class has been working together on a project which is not easily moved, then parents may not get a chance to see what their child is doing until there is an Open Evening or Parents' Evening. This may be months away, and by then the work may be damaged, broken up, or simply no longer of interest. With an IWB, any child can take home a print-out of the work they have been doing if they want to show it to their parents or talk to them about it. This facilitates parental involvement in project work, or in appreciating how much a child has improved in some particular aspect.

CHAPTER 3

Pedagogy

Research shows that effective use of ICT occurs when teachers realise it may need a new approach to pedagogy, and this applies equally to use of an IWB. Children still need their learning to be monitored and structured, and there still needs to be a clear focus on the subject learning. The main task for a teacher is not to familiarise themselves with the software or the equipment, but to understand how these can contribute to the lesson objectives.

Features of effective teaching include the following:

- making sure children are aware of the relevance of a lesson to what has gone before, or what is to come

- checking that the children have any prior knowledge required at the beginning of the lesson

- clear expectations

- a well-structured and well-paced lesson

- differentiation to ensure that there are tasks accessible to and appropriate for all children

- authentic learning tasks which are relevant and interesting for the children

- incorporating children's ideas throughout the planning stage of an activity as well as during it, to maximise children's ownership of what they do

- high-quality content

- maintaining the children's interest and suiting the needs of different types of learners through the use of a variety of teaching styles and resources

- using questions to find out how well the children understand what is going on and encouraging children to ask questions of their own

- allowing children to take some responsibility for their own learning by encouraging independent thinking and collaborative work.

I observed several excellent lessons in which the IWB was used to provide whole class teaching and discussion and differentiated activities for small groups of children, alongside other activities for the whole class, small groups and individuals. The IWB supported all these activities, providing variety and pace. The children clearly enjoyed their lessons. It was equally clear that they were learning, and that they were able to articulate what they were learning.

One example will suffice here. I watched a small group of Y2 children (aged 6–7 years) at the IWB with the teacher towards the end of a Maths lesson. They were using a program which provided numbers and an answer, but omitted the operation relating them. A typical question looked like this: $45 = 5$? 9. The children had to tap the correct symbol which would then be put between the 5 and the 9. If they were right, 'wonderful' or a similar expression of praise would result; if they were wrong, it was 'sorry, have another go'. The teacher encouraged the children to discuss together what they thought the operation should be, asking each other to justify their reasoning.

One girl, Melanie, hung back at the edge of the group, standing a little distance away, although the others were sitting close to the board. She did not take part in the discussions until the teacher asked her to come up to the board, and take the role of the teacher. To my surprise, she did so, asking the other children appropriate questions so that they chose the correct symbol and justified their choice. She then joined in with the rest of the group. Standing at the IWB, taking the part of the teacher, gave Melanie the confidence to become part of the group. Although she found Maths hard, asking questions of the others helped her to think about the reasoning needed to choose a symbol, so that she was then ready to join in with the group.

Was the IWB essential here? The program provided the children with all the numbers and symbols they needed, in a clear, colourful format, so they did not have to worry about writing or providing questions. This also made them far more independent of the teacher than they would normally be. The children clearly enjoyed the program far more than they would have enjoyed a worksheet with similar questions on it. Working as a small group, taking turns to be the 'teacher', helped them to focus on how a choice of symbol should be made, so that answering the questions was not random, but carefully thought through.

It is likely that teachers who are already demonstrating good practice will continue to show it in their teaching if and when they use an IWB. Such teachers certainly do not need an IWB to teach well. Working with an IWB may however prompt a teacher to rethink how a lesson is taught, rather than relying on tried and tested strategies. This may enable teachers to be more creative and innovative in how they present material, or in the extra resources they use.

Although IWB use cannot of itself make someone into a good teacher, it definitely has something to offer the different learning styles which children show. Our brains access information through visual, auditory and kinaesthetic sensory inputs. The range of different types of sensory stimulation which can be used with an IWB will benefit all types of learners. Visual learners can enjoy the colours, graphics, pictures, graphs, mind-maps and so on; kinaesthetic learners will appreciate videos and animations, and can touch and move things on the board; audio and video files can be used to supplement classroom discussion to stimulate auditory learners.

The board can be used to free children from the need to take notes or copy things down from the board. Notes can be taken at the board by a 'scribe' (not necessarily the teacher) during discussion and can then be saved and printed out if children need their own copy. If children have discussed with each other and the teacher how they are to set about a task, pace and focus may be better maintained by the children getting on with the task, rather than stopping to make notes on what is to be done.

IWB use can also help teachers to present their lessons in a structured way, with objectives made clear, and links to preceding material emphasised. Hyperlinks can be made to different activities, allowing differentiation and quick access to a variety of resources. Pace can be maintained since everything needed in a lesson can be made available at the click of an electronic pen or the tap of a finger. High-quality content and authentic tasks can be resourced in many different ways.

A lesson might start with a review of the material covered in the previous lesson, using the summary from the end of the previous lesson. A summary of what is to be done in this lesson, with learning objectives clearly stated could then follow. Open questions might come next to encourage discussion, and allow for questions and answers from the class. Once the teacher is ready for the children to move into small groups or individual activity, the whiteboard can be used to make sure everyone knows what they are to do, with appropriate demonstrations from the board. Towards the end of the lesson, children could present their work on the board for a whole class discussion of what has been found out or achieved during the lesson, and to summarise. This would then form the start of the next lesson, with the opportunity to go back over any aspect children had not properly grasped in the previous lesson.

None of this looks very startling or innovative, although it is clearly useful to be able to review previous material or to look ahead to what is coming. However, the actual content of the boards at any point could be very different from anything seen on a traditional whiteboard. The files used might contain video, photos, images, text, or sound. If an unexpected question highlighted the need to diverge from the initial teaching plan, the wealth of resources available on the IWB makes it much easier to react to that question immediately, instead of saying 'Good question! I'll come back to that.'

Using an IWB means that work in progress can be kept so that it is ready as a starting point the next time the class works on that particular topic. This facilitates projects which last longer than one lesson, since everything that is on the IWB can be saved, and printed out if required. There is no danger of it getting lost or being damaged, and everyone can have access to everything that has been done. Each child can take home the entire project if they want to, for further work or to share with parents.

Children particularly like the large image and the visual emphasis which the IWB encourages: several of the children I talked to commented on this. Certainly, the big screen helps children to focus, to maintain their attention, and to see text clearly. The effect of this on their learning should not be underestimated. However, if this is to be made effective, teachers need to be sure that everything is easily visible from the back of the classroom. This is very straightforward: it merely requires briefly viewing material from the back of the room. It will not take long for a teacher to become aware of the minimum size of font and images which show up clearly. If anything is too small, or if colours do not show up against each other, it is easy to make the necessary changes.

Teaching style

The IWB is often used for whole class teaching, or for working with groups of children around the board. Whole-class teaching has been emphasised by the three-part lesson structure, particularly at the beginning and the end of the lesson, and an IWB is ideal for this aspect of teaching, but it can also be used by small groups of children, or even individuals. It is a fallacy that the IWB can only be used for whole-class work, however. Indeed, some of the most effective learning involving an IWB that I observed was with small groups of children both with and without the teacher.

Figure 3.1 'Teacher' James taking questions from the 'class'

The IWB takes the place of the ordinary whiteboard or overhead projector at the front of the class for occasions when the teacher wants all the children focused on the same thing. For instance, the teacher can demonstrate how to redraft a piece of writing. Children can discuss how the content needs changing, if there are grammatical or spelling errors, and so on. The whole class can concentrate on the same piece of work in a way that is not possible in any other way. As Kate (aged 11) said: '[everyone is] learning the same thing at the same time'. Even if everyone is looking at the same piece of work on their tables, they will not necessarily all be looking at the same thing at the same time. Looking up and down also allows children to be distracted by something else going on in the room or outside, and can be difficult for children with very short attention spans.

The IWB is very useful for occasions when the class is brainstorming an activity. Someone (not necessarily the teacher) can write down suggestions as they occur, then when everyone has had their say, the suggestions can be tidied up, saved for another day, and/or printed out for everyone to work on.

Whether the IWB is used with a whole class or with a small group, it can and should be used by the children, to encourage them to contribute to the lesson. Children can come to the board to demonstrate something to the rest of the class. Sitting the children on the carpet in front of the board makes this particularly easy.

Figure 3.2 The 'class' agree with the answer Sam is about to put on the board

Even the youngest children can use the board, provided it is set at a height which makes it possible for them to reach, or there is a step which they can safely use. If children are sat at tables, it may be preferable to use a wireless keyboard, wireless mouse, or an IWB tablet or slate so that they can put things on the board without leaving their seats. This may be better than streams of children coming out in turn to put something on the board, leading to a slow pace and opportunity for distraction.

There is a risk that the IWB will encourage teachers to spend too long at the front, transmitting information or instructing the children, and not enough time letting them work individually or in small groups. Critics of IWB technology have claimed that it encourages direct instruction at the expense of children being actively involved in their own learning. If the IWB is used for long sessions of direct instruction, then teaching style should be reconsidered, as the novelty value of a board used in this way will soon wear off.

There is no reason why IWB use should contribute to the greater use of direct instruction than was previously the case, however. Indeed, one teacher I spoke to said she found more opportunities to involve the children, so that there was more participation than previously, and the children were keener to contribute. 'They will run the show if you let them,' she said. Tom (aged 11) agreed: 'They're good because you can do things with them as normally you would just have a teacher writing on the board, but with an IWB you all get a go.'

There are times when it may well be appropriate to spend longer working as a whole class. If the IWB encourages discussion and children are engaged in the topic then this may be justified. The balance of whole-class to individual time can be redressed another day, with a greater amount of time spent on individual work.

One very effective lesson I observed started with the whole group gathered in front of the IWB working together from a resource which the teacher had downloaded from a website she had discovered. After a while, the teacher changed to another resource, which was an interactive game on the same topic. Children took turns to come up to the board to use the pen to tap the answer they thought was correct. Others helped them, by suggesting answers.

Then most of the class returned to their tables to work on individual activities, involving paper and pencil work, or work with practical activities. A small group stayed on at the IWB to continue working on another resource.

Figure 3.3 A small group working at the IWB at a task chosen specifically for them

Once they knew what they were doing, they took turns on the computers to continue on their own, and another group came up to the IWB to work on yet another resource. In this way, the teacher was able to provide differentiated tasks for the class, with small groups using the IWB to familiarise themselves with a task before working individually on the computers or on paper and pencil tasks. As a result, the children at the computers knew exactly what they were doing, and no time was wasted. There were frequent changes of activity, so that everyone stayed on task. In total, there were five different activities going on in the room, three of which used the IWB or the computers. At the end of the lesson, the teacher used one of the activities again for the plenary session, then a different game which again the children enjoyed greatly.

Pace was maintained throughout the lesson, and children were able to work on activities which were appropriate to them. Enjoyment and motivation were also maintained throughout. Those who did not work individually or in a group at the IWB this time knew their turn would come another day. Providing so many different activities would have taken far longer without the IWB, and some of the activities could not have been provided without the use of computers and the internet.

Pace and depth of learning

All the teachers I interviewed who were already using an IWB agreed that it increased the pace of their lessons. One said: 'I can pull things up, refer back to things we did earlier. I'm not faffing around with pages in a flipchart. It's more accessible, and I can flip from one thing to another.' Another agreed, saying: 'It helps keep the pace up . . . It helps you to be more organised.'

Children's attention is not lost by having to clean the board, and start over again, losing what has gone before. Indeed, there may be far less need to write on the board at all. I asked Tim (aged 8) what he thought of the IWB. 'It's brilliant,' he said, 'I really like it.' When I asked why, he replied 'You don't have to erase stuff. You can save it.' Caroline (aged 11) agreed: 'They are good as you don't have to write on the board, it saves time . . .'

Because all the resources needed for a lesson can be prepared ahead of time, and presented on the IWB, time is saved in having children hand out books and find the right page, or in the teacher having to write up material, or draw diagrams. Everything is ready on demand, as in the lesson described in the previous section. This means that teachers can explain quickly and efficiently what they want the class to do, so that there is more time for children to work independently or in small groups, and for the teacher to discuss concepts with them, rather than give instructions. 'I can demonstrate what they will use, for example, email, Flexi-tree, Word editing, through example . . . I have all 33 watching me at once, instead of eight round a monitor, so it saves a lot of time,' said one teacher.

Depth of learning can also be increased. I observed a lesson with a mixed Y1/2 group (aged 5–7 years) in which the teacher used a PowerPoint presentation to help the children with telling the time. She said that it had only taken her about 20 minutes to prepare the presentation, and that the real advantage was that it enabled her to ask more differentiated questions than she would have been able to do otherwise. She started with a real clock, asking the children what the time was, what it would be in half an hour, and so on, moving the hands to demonstrate. In the presentation which followed, she showed clocks with the hands on, asking similar questions. She also showed clocks without any hands on, and got the children to come up to the board and demonstrate where the hands should be if it was, say, quarter to five. Once the question was answered correctly, she tapped the board, and hands flew onto the clock, accompanied by clapping and cheers, much to the children's delight.

In another lesson I observed, Y3 children (aged 7–8 years) were discussing various multiplication tables. They were using a 100-square on the IWB so that the children could take turns to mark the numbers in a given table. They then discussed together the patterns the marks made. 2's and 5's were obvious – the marked numbers went down the square in columns (there was a discussion of the difference between a row and a column at this point). Then they did the 8 times table, but a mistake was made, with 31 marked instead of 32.

'That's wrong!' said Tim. 'How do you know?' replied the teacher. 'Because all the other numbers are in the knight's move.' The teacher then asked him to explain what he meant, which he did, coming up to the IWB to demonstrate. He helped the rest of the class to see that the pattern was to go down a row, and then back two columns, and they then agreed that it should be 32. This gave a visual element to the abstract idea of multiplying two numbers. When they did the 11 times table next, everyone knew they were looking for a pattern, and no mistakes were made. Predicting the next number became easy. Not only were these children helped to revise and learn more about their multiplication tables (so much more fun than doing table tests), but they were learning about the importance of pattern in Maths.

Motivation

Experience so far has shown that IWB use can be motivating for children, although concerns have been expressed that this will decrease as IWBs become commonplace rather than a novelty. However, many teachers have commented on aspects of IWB use which are likely to remain motivating, even when the novelty has worn off. It would appear that children agree with this: 'I enjoy using the IWB . . . Without this lessons wouldn't be as [much] fun because you can use programs that make the lessons interesting and easier to understand' (Helen, aged 11 years). 'I think they are quite good and are easier to learn from because you can use

PowerPoint and other programs to look at the lesson in more detail' (Kathryn, aged 11). 'It is good because you can see things instead of having to imagine them; you can find out more because you are linked to a computer and have internet access . . .' (Fran, aged 11).

The classes I observed had been exposed to IWB use for some time, and there was no sign that the novelty was wearing off, or that they were becoming bored with them. Provided the teacher was using appropriate resources which the children found stimulating, their interest was maintained. The IWB is not just a single resource, but a whole host of resources, so there is no reason why they should have novelty value only.

Increased motivation can mean children stay on task better. In all the classes I observed, children stayed on task, and appeared to be enjoying their work. They responded well to use of the IWB, and enjoyed opportunities to display their own work on it, add their own comments, or contribute answers.

Inclusion

How's this for a way to recapture the interest of children who have become distracted? Open up a digital photo of the class (already in your files), open the spotlight tool, and move the spotlight so that it shows the child/children who are not paying attention. It won't be long before they are!

The IWB can help all children to feel part of a lesson, and to reduce occasions when a child feels that there is nothing for them in it. All the children I spoke to were in favour of lessons where the IWB was used, from the youngest (who were 6 years old) to the oldest (who were 11 years old). Laura said, 'I think it's really fun and useful.' Yasmin said she hated squeaky, annoying chalk. Jason liked the big screen: 'It's good for painting on. [They had recently had a lesson where they had used the software Paint.] It's like a big canvas.' Peter liked the National Numeracy Strategy resources, saying they were 'better than paper and pencil, you don't have to sharpen your pencil or control the pen.' Francis liked the fact that you could have videos, and Melanie liked it because it was like the computer and she loved her computer.

Comparing working at the IWB and at a laptop, Ellie said, 'It's better at the board. It's easier with the pen. The mouse is a bit fiddly' (although she was perfectly competent with the laptop mouse). Another group liked doing the multiplication game they were playing at the IWB rather than on a computer because of the big screen and the fact that it was easier to put the cursor in the right place with the IWB pen than on the computer.

IWB use can help teachers to provide greater support for children with special educational needs or who have become de-motivated. Where children have sight or hearing problems, greater use can be made of other aspects of the board's functionality. Children with visual difficulties can be supported by the use of sound files, including speech and music. Those with hearing difficulties will enjoy a greater use of visual material. The range of video, sound and picture files which can be used is huge, and the IWB allows instant access to any of these. Using these can keep children who do not enjoy writing involved.

Children for whom English is not their first language, or who have emotional and behavioural difficulties, may find using digital video helpful. Using video to record themselves, or to record role plays or stories they have written, can help children to talk about themselves and their experiences, which impacts on language use and development. It can also help children to express their feelings about difficult or emotional events. Creativity and collaboration are emphasised in projects like this, which can help children to establish better relationships with their peers and teachers. Video clips can be presented via the IWB to the rest of the class, or used as part of ongoing work using other media.

Children with mobility difficulties may be better served with mobile boards than those which are fixed to a wall. Access by children in wheelchairs might be easier, and the board can be set at different heights, according to need. Alternatively, an open space in front of the board might solve such access issues. Provided wires to equipment are securely taped down, they should not present a problem even with a mobile board.

The types of board which allow children to use their fingers rather than mouse pens are particularly good for children with special needs. Children could produce their own pictures to illustrate their work, using their fingers to draw on the board, or by importing clipart. Many boards have handwriting recognition, which could aid some children. They can write directly on the board with their fingers, and the handwriting recognition tool can then convert this to text. Even calibrating the board can become a learning opportunity: as one child touches the calibration points with a finger, the rest of the class can count the points.

PART 2

Getting Started

CHAPTER 4

Getting acquainted with the interactive whiteboard

Various attempts have been made to identify stages in the development of teachers' use of an IWB. One such schema identifies familiarisation, utilisation, integration, reorientation and evolution. A teacher goes through familiarisation when she first begins to find out what it can do. One teacher I interviewed was at this stage. She was keen to find out more, but found simple things were holding her back. These included not knowing how to turn the board on, having a book case of library books placed in front of it, and so on.

Utilisation occurs when a teacher starts to use the board in the classroom by replacing things they would have done previously without it. This may seem unnecessary use: surely ICT should only be used if there is some clear advantage to be gained from that use? Apart from helping teachers to reach higher stages, this stage may not be without its own benefits, however. The pace of lessons may increase, through the ready availability of other resources, or higher-order questions may be provoked by the ability to annotate over documents and save the contents for another day.

A real difference occurs when a teacher reaches the stage of integration. At this stage, teachers regard the board as a necessary part of their teaching resources, and would not consider being deprived of it. IWB use is incorporated into lesson planning across the curriculum. A teacher at this stage is excited by the possibilities the board offers. Several of the teachers I interviewed were at this stage. One, who had been using an IWB for about a term and a half, said that she found her board a 'necessity. It's so much simpler having everything unified.'

Teachers who have reached the stage of reorientation are prepared to show others how to use it, demonstrating how to use it in their lessons. Two of the teachers I interviewed were at this stage. One said that she had gained confidence through using the board, and that this was reflected in her teaching and how she was with the children throughout the day. She enjoyed giving presentations, enjoying the recognition this gave her school and herself personally.

Finally, those who reach the stage of evolution are the teachers who evolve new ways of presenting material across the curriculum. Such a teacher will integrate ideas and various electronic resources to meet the needs of all the children in her class, always looking out for new ideas, and new ways of exploiting the technology available to her so that she improves children's learning experiences.

However, this part of this book is for beginners. It describes how the IWB functions, and how to use it with commonly available software, such as Microsoft Word. In the following chapter, detailed instructions are given for carrying out common operations, such as saving and printing, moving from one application to another, and so on, in Word, Paint, Excel, PowerPoint and in IWB software.

Getting going

A good place to start with a new IWB is by opening an internet site or program with which the class is already familiar. This enables the novice to concentrate on operating the board, as the activity is one that is already well-known. Interactive games gain from being displayed to the whole class on the IWB, and these might provide a good first step. It helps if the website or the program has been opened prior to the start of the lesson, so that a tap or click will bring it up, ready for use. Accessing websites can be time-consuming, so saving websites you like in 'Favourites' where they can be found again quickly is useful.

Displaying resources is helped if the toolbars are not visible when they are not needed. If a website is viewed through Internet Explorer, tapping F11 on the keyboard will remove the toolbars at the top of the page, making the content much clearer. Tapping it again will bring the toolbars back. Many other documents can be viewed Full Screen, which is normally to be found through the top toolbar: View>Full Screen will remove all the toolbars. When a document is in Full Screen view, there should be a small floating toolbar, which can be moved to a convenient place on the screen. Clicking or tapping on this will restore the normal view.

Annotation tools

The next step might be to use the special annotation tools, which are provided in the IWB software, with an internet site or familiar resource. Most boards will provide many different tools, but the basic ones to try out first are:

- pen

- highlighter

- eraser

- undo and redo

- clear all annotations

- 'camera' tool.

A particular type of IWB might not have all these. It is likely to have several others, but these are a good basic set to start with.

Any or all of these tools can be used with any piece of software, not just with the IWB's own software.

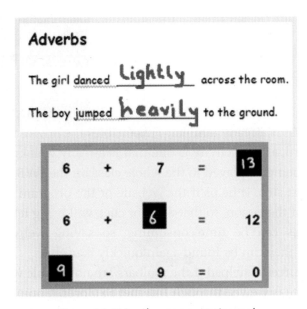

Figure 4.1 Using the pen annotation tool

The pen tool has been used in Figure 4.1 to annotate a Word and an Excel document. In the top image, the pen tool has been used to fill in the gaps in the sentences. In the lower image an Excel spreadsheet, which generates random numbers for basic arithmetic practice (files like this can be seen in Chapter 8), has answers written in white on black squares, using the pen tool. Figure 4.1 shows that the pen tool can be used with a number of different colours and in different widths. Similarly the highlighter and eraser can be changed according to need.

Using 'fill the gap' questions like these on an ordinary whiteboard would require time spent beforehand, writing out the questions. With an interactive whiteboard, the document is prepared as part of the lesson preparation and saved for use whenever required. More questions can be prepared than will be needed, so that examples can be chosen as required. The spreadsheet has the added advantage that it uses random numbers which can be changed at the touch of a key, so that a new set of questions is available for the class to answer whenever needed.

Both these images were captured using the IWB 'camera' tool. This tool allows a picture of anything on the computer screen to be taken and inserted into any document in any piece of software.

Creating templates and worksheets

It is very easy to create illustrations from drawings, photos or clipart with an IWB and this may give you many ideas for making up your own templates and worksheets. Anything that can be produced on an IWB can be saved for future use, or printed out and duplicated for the class. IWB software has a number of backgrounds already available (see some examples in Figure 4.2), and others can be added to these.

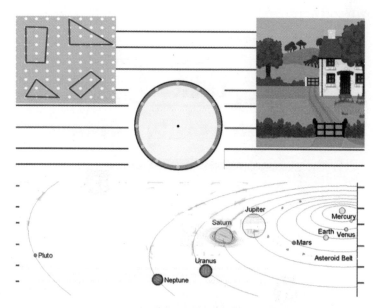

Figure 4.2 Some backgrounds available in IWB software

Presentation software

IWBs allow the use of two different types of presentation software. All types of IWB can be used for PowerPoint displays. IWB software also provides its own type of presentation software (the 'whiteboard'). Both these types of software enable teachers to produce their own resources, containing as many slides or pages as desired.

Slides/pages in these presentations can have special backgrounds or designs to create a professional look. They can also have hyperlinks embedded in them to other files, including sound and video files, or have pictures and photos inserted into them. PowerPoint also allows special effects to be used. It takes longer to learn how to create an effective presentation than to use the annotation tools, but a good presentation provides an excellent environment for innovative use of the IWB.

IWB software enables a teacher to display bright, accurate, attractive pictures and graphs. Some IWBs also allow shapes to be rotated and reflected. Displaying coins on the IWB is much easier for children to see than real coins, and it saves having to make large versions for whole class work (see Figure 4.3). Shapes can be moved across the page for sorting activities. Pages can be produced with handwriting lines embedded, ready for children to write. Scenes can be displayed for imaginative work and storytelling. Musical instruments could be shown with linked sound files so children could hear them playing.

Figure 4.3 Coins and notes from the IWB resources

IWB presentations also provide a way of making other resources accessible to the whole class. Old worksheets and transparencies can be scanned into the computer, then brightened up by converting black and white text to bold, colourful text on a coloured background, with additional pictures added. Internet sites which have text too small to be seen from the back of the classroom or where there is a lot of irrelevant material can be transformed into presentations (see Chapter 8 for an example).

Creating presentations is probably the most time-consuming aspect of using an IWB. Like everything else, however, practice makes perfect, or at least means that interesting lesson resources are much quicker to make. The bonus is that once a resource has been made, it can be permanently saved for future use.

When creating a presentation, it is as well to avoid the temptation to make it say everything. It is better to leave gaps, to have open questions, unannotated diagrams, empty maps, and so on, so that there is room for the children and teacher together to fill the spaces. Hyperlinks can allow a lesson to take off in different ways, rather than simply following a linear path. Leaving room for children to participate in a presentation and using links allows different pathways to be followed, depending on where class discussion goes on a given day.

Presentations require visual issues to be carefully considered. IWBs are meant to give excellent visual display, but this will not occur if there is bright sunlight shining on the board. A dark coloured background may help, with pale colours for text and images. Lack of contrast can also be a reason for visibility problems: deep colours do not show up against other deep colours, and pale colours do not show up against other pale colours. It is a good idea to have a deep colour for the background or the text and a pale colour for the other. Colours which are opposite each other in the colour spectrum show up well against each other. Green/red is a special case, however, as there may be children with green/red colour blindness in the class. Many children with dyslexia find a pale yellow or cream against a dark blue, or *vice versa*, helps them to see things more clearly. Other children with dyslexia may have other colour schemes they prefer; if there is such a child in a class, the teacher can make sure that colour schemes facilitate this child's visual abilities, rather than the reverse.

Use of additional ICT

Access to a scanner somewhere on the school's network is extremely useful. This allows children's work on paper or in exercise books to be scanned in for display. It also means that text can be scanned into the computer and displayed on the IWB for a class to read together. Such text can be made as large and colourful as required, and children's attention can be drawn to particular words using the highlighter.

Video files and sound files can be added to most presentation software. This means that video can be incorporated without the need to find a TV set and video player, but can instead be played directly from the IWB. Digital video clips could be made by the children, or could show them doing a role play or presenting information. Such resources could add a completely new dimension to a lesson. Children can make their own sound files as well as using those available on the computer. Digital cameras can be used to add photos taken of or by the children around the school, or on trips out of school. Using additional ICT in this way will not only add hugely to the interest of resources, but will also give children ownership of their lesson materials.

CHAPTER 5

Basic operations

Many of the techniques needed to use an IWB are those required for common applications such as Word, PowerPoint and Paint. In this chapter, the basics of how to use such software are given together with details on using IWB software for ACTIVprimary boards and SMARTboards. The purpose of this chapter is to cover the most important technical details in one place so that resources can be described in Part 3 without too much repetition.

Common operations

Generally speaking, Microsoft Office applications (such as Word, PowerPoint and Excel), MS Paint and SMARTboard notebooks operate in the same way, whereas Promethean ACTIVprimary has some differences. In the following sections, you can assume that all these applications act in the way described, unless a different method of performing an operation in a particular application is given. If you are unsure what a particular icon does, hover the mouse above it for a few seconds. The name of the icon should show, and often this will be sufficient to explain what it does.

Orienting the board

Before you start using your IWB, you will need to orient it. This is a way of ensuring that the point of the pen/finger corresponds to the mouse arrow. You will need to find out how this is done on your board from the Users Guide, but generally a series of points will show on the board, which have to be tapped or clicked in a given sequence.

During use the board may become un-orientated, particularly if it is not fixed to a wall. This will become apparent, if clicking or tapping on an icon fails to operate it, and you can see that the mouse arrow is not in the same place as the point of the pen or fingertip. Quickly re-orientating the board solves the problem, and is a task children are quite capable of doing when necessary.

Saving and printing

Almost all software applications use the same symbols for common operations like saving and printing. Saving and printing are normally found in the File menu (File is usually the left-hand menu on the top toolbar). Alternatively, click on the icon that looks like a floppy disk to save, or press Ctrl (Control) and S on the keyboard. To print, click on the icon that looks like a printer, or press Ctrl P on the keyboard. As with much of what follows, ACTIVprimary software is a little different. It does not have these icons always visible, nor do the standard keyboard shortcuts work, although many of the icons used are the same as in other applications. To save or print a flipchart, click on the 'Promethean man' at the top left of the vertical toolbar. This opens up the 'Teacher Tools'. The third icon from the left is the 'save' icon and the fourth from the left is the 'print' icon (see Figure 5.1).

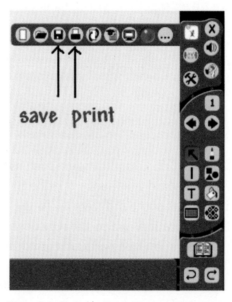

Figure 5.1 Saving and printing in ACTIVprimary

When saving a document in ACTIVprimary, to keep it in a folder other than the default folder (which is part of the ACTIVprimary folders) use the Windows icon (left-hand icon at the top of the box which appears after clicking on the Save icon) to navigate to another folder of your choice.

Moving from one application to another

One of the advantages of using an IWB is that you can move very quickly between computer applications. This means you can access several different resources as often as you want. Try opening two or three different documents: you will see the taskbar right at the bottom of the screen showing them all. The application that is currently active is a darker colour than any other applications that are open. To move from one to another, click on the required tab.

ACTIVprimary software can be accessed by clicking on its tab on the taskbar, but a different method is needed to return to a different application from ACTIVprimary. Click on the top left-hand icon on the vertical toolbar (which shows a 'Promethean man'). Selecting this brings up the Teacher tools. The third icon from the right, called Desktop capture, allows you to go back to your desktop so that the taskbar is visible again.

Copy/cut and paste

Copying or cutting then pasting text or pictures, perhaps from one page to another or from one application to another, is a very common operation. Cutting removes an object from its current application, copying leaves it in its current application. In most applications, this can be done either by using the menus on the top toolbar, or by using keyboard shortcuts. To cut, select what you want to remove, by clicking or tapping on it, then either click on Edit>Cut from the top toolbar or press Ctrl (Control) and X on the keyboard. To copy, select what you want to copy, then either click on Edit>Copy or press Ctrl and C on the keyboard. This either removes or copies the highlighted material to the 'clipboard'. Once something is on the clipboard, it is accessible from any application in Windows.

To paste into another application, or into the same application in a different place, go to the point where you want the cut or copied material to go, and either click on Edit>Paste or use Ctrl V on the keyboard. You should find the text or picture in its new position.

The only application where this procedure does not work is ACTIVprimary. Start by cutting or copying the object from the other application, then return to the ACTIVprimary flipchart. Next, click on the Promethean man on the vertical toolbar, then on the second Promethean man (second icon from the right on the Teachers tools). This has the effect of putting you into Design Mode (see below), and makes the border around the main Promethean man turn red (a reminder that you are in Design Mode). Then, with the mouse arrow pointing at the flipchart page, right click on the pen or on the keyboard. A pop-up menu will appear, giving the option of pasting the copied object from the clipboard onto the flipchart. To copy or cut an item from a flipchart, right click on it, and use the Copy option from the pop-up menu, then go to the other application and paste it in the required place.

Inserting pictures

Inserting photos, picture files, clip-art, and so on, is done in the same way in most applications. Either copy the picture and paste it into the new document as described above, or use the Insert menu on the top toolbar. Clicking on Insert>Pictures gives a range of alternatives. Selecting Clip Art opens clip-art files and a picture can then be opened in the document, or dragged into it. Clicking on From Files opens a box which will allow you to open any picture files you may have on your computer. Another alternative is to add a picture directly from a scanner or digital camera, and again there is an option for this.

Once you have inserted the picture into the document, it can be resized by dragging the 'handles' on the sides and corners of the picture. Using just the handles on the corners will maintain the width:height ratio of the picture. Dragging on either of the side handles will distort the picture. The SMARTboard is slightly different, in that there is only one handle to drag on, which is to be found at the bottom right of the picture. Dragging this diagonally maintains the width:height ratio, while dragging it horizontally or vertically distorts it.

Again, the only software which is significantly different is ACTIVprimary. The easiest way to incorporate a picture from outside ACTIVprimary into a flipchart is to copy it from the original source and then to paste it into the flipchart in Design Mode, as described above. A wide range of clip-art and images is also available from the Resource Library in ACTIVprimary. Accessing these is described below.

Inserting sound and video files

To create reasonable sound or video files, you need a fast computer with a sound card, and software such as Windows Media Player. You will also need a good microphone. Poor quality audio is a common problem in sound and video files, and is usually due to a poor quality microphone. To make a video file, you will need a digital video camera. Follow the instructions with your camera to produce a file which you can then attach to your resource. Attaching files to presentations is described below. Sound and video files can be attached to PowerPoint files and to many IWB software files. Attaching sound files is described in detail in Chapter 7, where sound is used to enhance a class book.

SMARTboard software contains its own sound/video recorder. The sound recorder can be used directly to create sounds which can then be attached to a notebook. This is described in Chapter 7. The video recorder can be used to create a video of everything that happens on a SMARTboard, whatever application is in use. This means you can produce a video of a PowerPoint file, say, complete with annotations produced using the SMART tools, which can then be played back using either the SMART Video Player or Windows Media Player. The SMART recorder is straightforward to operate. It can be accessed by tapping on the SMARTboard icon on the desktop or in Start>Programs, then selecting Recorder.

This will open a toolbar, with Record, Pause and Stop options. Further options can be found by tapping the Options tab on the toolbar. These allow you to select the sound video quality you want, amongst other things.

Using common software

Word

Word, from Microsoft Office, is a form of word-processing software. Its main use is in processing text, and in Chapter 7 classroom resources are discussed which make use of this. You can also insert pictures and draw in Word. To insert a picture from the clip-art on your computer, or from a file of your own, go to the top toolbar, and click on Insert>Picture and then select an option. This also allows you to insert WordArt.

To draw in Word, you will first need to check that the Drawing toolbar is open. If you cannot see a toolbar with Draw on the left-hand end (probably just above the Windows taskbar at the bottom of the screen), right click on any toolbar. A pop-up menu will open which gives you the option to open any other toolbar. Select the Drawing toolbar. Wherever the Drawing toolbar opens, it can be dragged to the top, bottom, or either side, whichever is most convenient, by left clicking just to the left of Draw and then dragging.

The Draw toolbar has icons for many different shapes that can be inserted, and there is also a free-hand pen. In addition, this toolbar includes icons which connect to WordArt, clip-art and picture files. Other icons allow the colour and thickness of lines to be changed, and shapes to be filled with colour. Text can be inserted into drawings by using the Textbox icon (which has a capital A in the left-hand corner and text around it).

PowerPoint

PowerPoint is an extremely useful tool for anyone using an IWB. Many ideas can be put into a PowerPoint presentation, giving them that professional look. Text, pictures, graphs, tables, sounds and video can all be added to slides. Slides can also be annotated during a presentation with a freehand pen available in the PowerPoint software, which could be useful to those using just a data projector. There is not nearly as much choice of pen colour as with IWB annotation tools, however, and the width cannot be changed. These annotations cannot be saved either. A wide range of special effects can be used to animate a presentation, although too many could be distracting.

It is a good idea to start preparing a PowerPoint presentation by setting up a master for the slides, called the Slide Master. This allows all colours and text for-matting to be chosen at the start, so that everything created follows the chosen scheme. To do this, go to View>Master>Slide Master on the top toolbar. A few basic rules are worth taking into consideration at this stage: using a strong colour for both text and background does not work very well, neither does using a pale colour for both. Red can be a difficult colour either for text or the background. It is better to mix a strong colour and a pale one, so that there is a good contrast between colours, such as cream on dark blue, or dark green on a very light yellow. You can use a Design Template by clicking on Format>Apply Design. This will give you a range of designs which you can choose to give your slides a particular look or style.

If you would rather sort out your own design, Click on Format>Slide Design (Slide Colour Scheme in earlier versions of PowerPoint). You will be offered a few colour schemes, but you can change any of these to your own colour scheme, by clicking on Custom, and changing the colours in each of the boxes. To see what it looks like, click on Preview, which will show you this colour scheme on your current slide. When you are happy with your design, click on Apply to All, to put it onto all your slides.

You can change the colour and texture of your background separately, by clicking on Format>Background on the top toolbar. Click on the right-hand arrow by the colour bar below your colour scheme – you will see your current colours displayed, plus the options More Colours and Fill Effects. Fill Effects allows you to choose a textured or patterned background.

Once you have decided on your design, colour scheme, fonts, and so on, it is time to create a new slide. Go to Insert>New Slide on the top toolbar, or use Ctrl M on the keyboard. You will be offered a choice of format for the slide – do you want a heading and bullet-points, pictures only, text and pictures? Drawings can also be made on PowerPoint slides using the Drawing toolbar, which is the same as that in Word.

PowerPoint opens in Slide view, which allows you to create and edit slides. Slideshow view is needed to display the presentation. For this go to the View menu (on the top toolbar), and then select Slideshow. Alternatively, use the right-hand icon (which looks a bit like a camera) on the bottom left of the slides, just above the Start button, as shown in Figure 5.2.

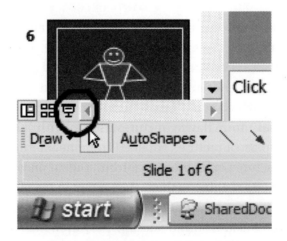

Figure 5.2 Slideshow icon in PowerPoint

To run the display, click the mouse once, or tap once on the screen with the pen or your finger. Clicking or tapping on the screen again moves the presentation on to the next slide. To return to the previous slide, or go elsewhere in the presentation, press the slide number on the keyboard if you know it, followed by the ENTER key. Otherwise, press the A key or the = key on the keyboard, or move the mouse to the bottom left of the screen. An arrow should appear in the bottom left corner of the screen. Click on this, and a range of options will appear, including slide navigation. This menu also includes the annotation pen. The Esc key (escape) will take you back to Slide view.

When giving a presentation, you may want to show bullet points or pictures on a slide sequentially, rather than all at once. To do this, go to Slide Show on the top toolbar, and select Custom Animation. Depending on which version of PowerPoint you are using, you will be given a new menu or a box which allows you to select from a range of different ways in which material can be displayed – you may want to experiment with this. Once you have selected an effect, you have the opportunity to accompany it with a sound of some kind, and/or have the text dim when a new bullet point is shown. PowerPoint contains a library of sounds and videos, which can be accessed from the top toolbar using Insert>Movies and Sounds. You can also use this to access sound and video files of your own or to record a new sound file.

On a SMARTboard, there is a specific means for saving annotations made on a PowerPoint slide using the SMARTboard pens. If you do nothing, the annotations will disappear when you continue with the presentation, and you will not be able to restore them. To save them, press the menu button in the Slide Show toolbar which appears when a pen is removed from the pen tray. Clear Annotations will remove all annotations from a slide; Restore Annotations will put them back. Save Annotations to PowerPoint will save your annotations so that they become part of the PowerPoint slide. Settings>Auto-Save Annotations on Slide Advance will save all annotations on the slide at the point where it is advanced to the next slide. A third alternative is to select Capture to Notebook. This saves the annotation plus the background slide into the current notebook, or a new one if none is open. Choosing the Print option will print the annotation and the slide content, but will not save the annotation.

Paint

Many resources benefit from having pictures used to illustrate them. These might be digital photos, clip-art or pictures obtained from the internet. However, it is not always best to use pictures in their original form. Digital photos are often very big files, with areas that add nothing to the main content of the photo. There are many different software packages for editing photos and pictures, and if you have a digital camera, you may have such a package. However, Microsoft Paint, which is normally available in Windows, is quite adequate for basic editing.

Paint can be found from the Start button in Programs>Accessories>Paint. If you are unfamiliar with it, start by opening a new document in Paint. The top toolbar gives menus similar to those found in Word. However, there is also a left-hand toolbar containing icons specific to drawing packages, as shown in Figure 5.3.

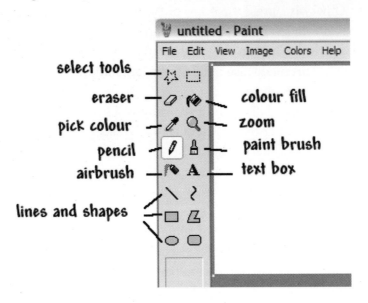

Figure 5.3 Tools available in Paint

Figure 5.3 shows the toolbars and icons in Paint, together with the names of the icons. Most are self-explanatory, and a little experimentation will show what they do. If the drawing canvas which appears on opening a new document is not the right size, there are 'handles' on the bottom right corner and the right and bottom sides which can be used to change the size of the canvas. If the image is the wrong size or the wrong orientation, this can be changed using the Image menu on the top toolbar. This is often useful for digital photos which may be very large, or turned sideways. To crop a picture, select the area you want with one of the Select tools from the left-hand icons. You can then either copy and paste it into a new canvas, or drag it away from the background. Moving the handles in will then remove the unwanted background.

The butterfly in Figure 5.4 was created in Paint by using the Curved Line tool (draw a straight line from the starting point to the finishing point of the curve, then use the mouse to click where the centre of the line should be, and click again when you are finished), the Ellipse tool, and the Fill tool. The left-hand side of the butterfly was drawn, then copied (Ctrl C) and pasted back into the document (Ctrl V). This was then flipped using Image>Flip/Rotate. Because you can flip and rotate, and stretch and skew images in Paint, it has many uses in a variety of curriculum areas for producing images. It can also be used to see what happens when shapes are rotated or reflected.

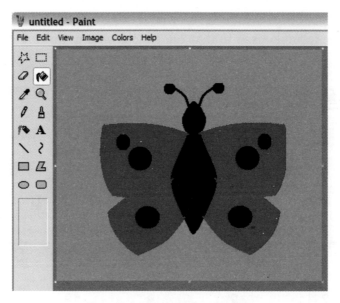

Figure 5.4 Image produced in Paint

Excel

Microsoft Excel does not seem to be used much in primary schools, teachers perhaps feeling it is more appropriate to their secondary colleagues. This is a great pity, as there are many ways in which Excel can be used to enhance the curriculum in primary schools. Some ideas are given in Chapter 8.

If you know how to use Word, then you will also know many of the basics of Excel; in particular, the top toolbar is very similar. However, where Word provides a blank sheet of paper for text, Excel is made up of 'cells', defined by rows labelled numerically and columns labelled alphabetically. Text or numbers can be put into any cell. Excel can therefore be used to keep information in table form.

It is also very good for doing calculations. Try putting a calculation into a cell and pressing ENTER. Surprisingly, perhaps, nothing happens. Now try the same calculation, but with an '=' sign first. This tells Excel to treat the figures as a calculation, rather than just a piece of text, and an answer will be produced. (* is used for multiplication and / for division.)

Now suppose you want to produce a multiplication table. It is not necessary to put in every calculation separately. Put a 1 in the top left-hand cell, labelled A1. In the second cell, A2, type in =A1 + 1 (the A1 can also be entered by clicking on cell A1). Pressing the ENTER key should then make a 2 appear in cell A2. Go back to cell A2, and put the mouse over the bottom right-hand corner of the cell, so that a black cross appears. Now drag the mouse downwards until you reach row 10. When you let go, you should see a column of figures from 1 to 10. Next put a 9 in cell B1, and drag down again. This time you should see a column of 9's. Finally, put =A1*B1 in cell C1. Drag down again, and the 9 times table should appear, as in Figure 5.5. Notice that cell C7 containing the result of 7 × 9 is selected in Figure

5.5. Above alphabetic row headings, in what is known as the formula bar (it has *fx* on the left), the formula used in that cell for calculating the answer of 63 is displayed, A7*B7.

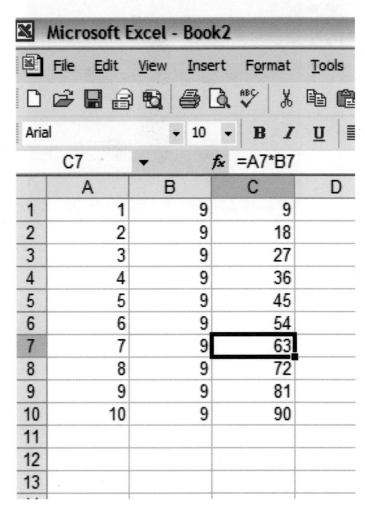

Figure 5.5 A multiplication table created in Excel

At the moment, our spreadsheet does not look very inviting, but a little formatting can make a considerable difference. The size, font and colour of the figures and the colour of the background can all be changed using the icons on the main toolbar. Examples of spreadsheets that can be used in the primary Maths lesson are given in Chapter 8, and there is more detail there of how to do this, and how using random numbers can give an endless supply of resources.

CHAPTER 6

IWB software

As we have already seen, every IWB has its own software which can also be used to great effect in producing classroom resources. This is what makes an IWB different from simply using a data projector and a computer. Two different types of IWB software are discussed here: the ACTIVprimary flipchart, produced by Promethean, and the SMARTboard notebook. Promethean have other versions of their software, but the ACTIVprimary interface has been designed specifically for primary schools.

SMARTboard notebook

Getting started

The main things you will probably want to do to start with are to move to a new page, insert freehand or typed text or a picture, and navigate round pages you have created, then save and retrieve your document. If you are opening up the software, Open Notebook will give you a new notebook. If you want to create a new notebook at any other time, use the keyboard shortcut Ctrl N or File>New from the top toolbar menu. To open a notebook you have previously saved, click on File>Open from the top toolbar menu, or use the keyboard shortcut Ctrl O. Other useful Windows keyboard shortcuts which can be used with a SMARTboard are Ctrl Z, which will undo your last action, Ctrl Y which repeats your last action, Ctrl S which saves the document currently open and Ctrl P which prints the document currently open (these can all be used in Microsoft applications as well). Ctrl C and Ctrl V to copy and paste are also useful. Other keyboard shortcuts are shown in the drop-down menus on the top toolbar.

Figure 6.1 shows the icons which provide a new page, or navigate back and forth between pages. The first two are self-explanatory, the third deletes the currently open page, and the fourth produces a blank page. To access any of these tools, simply tap on the icon.

Figure 6.1 Some SMARTboard icons

The toolbar

Open up a new SMARTboard notebook. You may see a toolbar along the top, which looks very like the kind of thing you would expect in Word. Alternatively, you may see a toolbar along the left-hand side, with just the main menus along the top. You can change from one to the other by using the View menu – click on View>Simple toolbar. If this is selected, there will be a simple toolbar vertically along the left-hand side of the screen. If it is not selected, there will be a more complex toolbar with more options horizontally along the top of the screen. The simple toolbar may be more appropriate for use in class, so that children can reach the icons easily. In preparation, however, it is probably preferable for the teacher to use the more complex toolbar.

The Floating Tools

The Floating Tools can be used with any application, not just with notebooks. To open them, if they do not open automatically, go to Control Panel>Floating tools tray.

Figure 6.2 SMARTboard floating tools

Figure 6.2 shows an enlarged collection of Floating Tools. The top two rows are the default option. To add extra tools, drag them onto the tool tray; a new row can be opened by dragging the tools on the left-hand drag bar. To remove a tool, drag it into the trash can. The tools which have been added here include in the third row three keys from the keyboard (not terribly useful, since they require the onscreen keyboard for other keys). The fourth row contains the Spotlight, the Screen Capture and Area Capture tools, and the onscreen keyboard. The fifth row contains the Select arrow, the Undo tool and a tool which opens up a new notebook.

Annotations on a notebook page will be saved with the notebook. Annotations over other software, such as Word, Paint or PowerPoint can also be saved. Lifting a pen from the tray makes a floating toolbar appear, which contains options allowing you to save your annotations to a notebook, or as an object in the software currently open. Such objects can then be edited using the Microsoft Draw editing toolbar. Alternatively, the Screen Capture tool (see below) can be used to copy any annotations either to a notebook or to the Windows clipboard. From the clipboard, they can be pasted into any application desired.

Using a notebook with the pens from the tray

In addition to the Floating Tools, there are four pens in the pen tray which are automatically linked to a particular colour. The colour and width of the line produced can be changed by tapping on the pen icon on the Floating Tools. This will open up a box in which the desired colour and width can be selected. The pen will automatically change back to its pre-set colour when it is replaced in the pen tray. To erase freehand writing, use the eraser from the pen tray. Like the pens, the width of the erasing line can be changed via the Floating Tools.

Handwriting can be changed to typed text. To do this, select the handwriting you want to convert; there should be a letter A in the top right corner. Tapping on this will give alternatives from which you can then select whichever corresponds most closely to what was written. If this is still not quite right, it can be edited, by tapping on the text and then using the onscreen keyboard or the computer keyboard. Selecting freehand writing also allows you to use Edit>copy from the top toolbar to copy it as it stands, or Edit>Copy as text to copy it as typewritten text. Figure 6.3 shows a page with a picture inserted, and freehand text, some of which has already been converted to text, and some which is about to be converted to text ('This page'). As you can see, the text converter did not do a particularly good job here. You will have to decide whether it is worth converting handwritten text to typewritten text this way, or whether it is easier to type in the text from scratch. This will probably depend on your handwriting, and how easy it is for the software to recognise it, but it could be useful when brainstorming an idea in class, so that notes can be produced afterwards.

Using a notebook in preparation (without the board)

SMARTboard software can be used on a computer without the board attached, which is useful for preparation. When a notebook is opened without the board

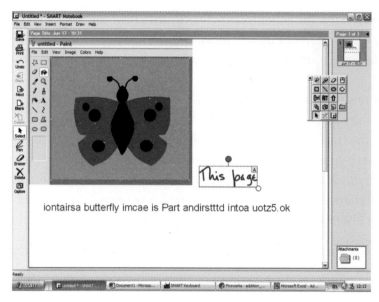

Figure 6.3 Handwriting recognition

attached to the computer, a watermark shows across the page, which will disappear when the notebook is used with the board. The Floating Tools cannot be used without the board: to insert freehand text in preparation, use the pen tool which can be accessed either by using the Pen icon on the toolbar, or from the Draw>Pen menu. The eraser does not work if you are working from the computer only. Freehand text has to be removed in the same way as any other object on a notebook page. To remove several letters or words, pull a selection box around it and then use the Delete key on the keyboard. To remove just one or two letters, use Ctrl Z or use the Undo icon to remove the last action. Handwriting recognition does not work without the board, but most other operations can be carried out with or without the board.

Typed text

To insert typed text, simply start typing anywhere on a notebook page. Text can then be moved wherever you want by dragging. It can be edited by tapping on it, inserting the cursor where you want to edit, and adding something else, or by selecting what is wrong and over-typing. Text boxes can be resized, which will affect the layout of the text, but will not affect the font size. To change the font size of text, select the text, then click on it again. This will show a cursor in the text box. Highlight the text you want to resize, then use Format>Font to choose a new font type, size or colour.

Resizing and rotating

Items on a flipchart page, such as text or pictures, can be moved, resized and rotated. Tap on a piece of text or a picture. You will see a dotted line around the object, with a white circle at the bottom right and a green circle above the top middle of it. An object can be moved by dragging it. To resize it, pull the white circle at the bottom right. You can pull this diagonally which maintains the height:width ratio, or vertically or horizontally, which distorts it. The green circle above a selected object allows rotation in either direction.

Adding pictures

To insert a picture from the clip-art included in the software, go to Insert>Clipart and select the category you want. To insert a photo or a picture directly from a Scanner, go to Insert>Picture from Scanner. To insert a photo or picture you already have on your computer, choose Insert>Clipart, and instead of selecting from the folders shown, navigate up through the directories to the one you want. In each case, once you have the picture you want, select Open. You may find that your picture is too big for the page. In this case, use the Grow Page button at the bottom of the page until you can see the bottom of the picture. Then tap on the picture to select it, and use the bottom right-hand corner circle to pull it to the size you want. You can also drag the picture to place it where you want. To remove a picture, or any other object, select it, and then press Delete on the keyboard.

Figure 6.4 A typical SMARTboard page

Figure 6.4 shows a new page created with text and a picture from the SMARTboard clipart. This page has been prepared without the board attached, and the watermark can be seen; this will disappear when a board is connected to the computer. The simple toolbar can be seen on the left. At the bottom of the screen, the other applications open are displayed on the taskbar, so that navigating from one application to another is just a matter of tapping on these tabs. At the top right, the two pages so far created in this document are displayed, and at the bottom right there is a folder for attachments, which is currently empty. Once you have created your new notebook, you will need to save it, and possibly to print it. The Save icon is at the top of the left-hand toolbar, and the Print icon is just below it.

Menu options

The **File menu** contains save and print options as in Word and similar applications. To make and save your own page templates, save them as a template (File>Save Page as Template). You can save background colours as well as objects on the page such as sets of handwriting lines or maps. This option was used in a number of the English resources discussed in Chapter 7, and an example can be seen later in Figure 6.6.

The **Edit menu** contains options for deleting pages, copying and pasting, again as in Word.

Options not yet mentioned which are available in the **View menu** include Whiteboard, Page Sorter, Attachments, and Full Screen. In Whiteboard, most of the screen is available as a whiteboard as in Figure 6.4, but small versions of each page created can be seen vertically on the right. These can be used to navigate from one page to another. Page Sorter view shows these small versions of the pages. In either view, pages can be moved to change their order by dragging them to a new position. In Attachments view, any files attached to a notebook can be seen. These can also be seen in Whiteboard view, on the bottom right of the screen. Full Screen is useful where you want to display a presentation without the distraction of the toolbars, or where you need a bit more space to show all of a page, as it removes the toolbars and page sorter from around the whiteboard. To return to Whiteboard view, just tap on the floating Full Screen icon and select End Full Screen, or use the Escape key on the keyboard. View>Screen Shade provides a screen across the page, which can be pulled down so that items only become visible as you determine.

The 'camera' icon on the toolbar and on the Floating Tools, corresponding to View>Screen Capture, is extremely useful. You can use this tool either in the notebook or in any other software you are using, including internet pages, which makes it an easy way to incorporate pictures and text from other applications. Tapping on this produces a new floating toolbar, with options of Area, Window, Screen, and a box to select for Save Pictures to a New Page. Selecting this box will mean your 'photo' is printed on a new page; not selecting it will mean that your 'photo' is printed on the current page. Area enables you to draw out an area which you wish to 'photograph'. Selecting Window means the whole of the visible area, you are working on will be 'photographed', but not the toolbars around the outside of the active window. Selecting Screen means that the whole screen, including the active window, the toolbars, everything, will be 'photographed'. If you want to copy a 'photo' to another application, just select it, then use Cut or Copy and Paste from the Edit menu, or use the Ctrl X or C and Ctrl V shortcuts on the keyboard.

There is also a Screen Capture icon on the Floating Tools. This works in the same way as described above, with options of Capture the Screen and Capture an Area. Both put the picture onto a new page of a notebook, however, without giving you the option of putting it onto the current page.

The screen shade icon on the more complex toolbar (but not found on the simple toolbar), corresponding to View>Screen Shade, is the Show/Hide Screen Shade. Tap it to use it, tap it again to remove it. This gives a shade over the Window which can be pulled up and down to hide and reveal objects on a page, as you might do with a piece of paper over an overhead projector transparency.

The **Insert menu** allows you to insert clip-art and pictures, or other files, into your notebooks. It also enables you to create hyperlinks on your pages, so that clicking on these links automatically calls up another file. This could be a picture, a video or any other resource you wanted to link into your notebook. Also on the Insert menu is an option allowing you to use a page template. There are templates in the software already created for use, and if you explore this option you will find square grids, lined paper, blank clocks, background scenes and so on. The Math section includes a protractor and ruler, which can be rotated, coins, and 10, 20 and 100 squares. There are maps of the UK, the continents, and the world in the Map folder, and many other useful resources for all curriculum areas.

Objects, such as pictures or text, can be dragged from other software into a SMARTboard notebook and *vice versa* via the Windows taskbar. To copy the object, rather than removing it from its current location, first hold down the Ctrl key. Then select the object, and drag it down to the bottom taskbar, to the notebook icon. This will open the notebook, so that you can drag the object up onto the page. This can also be done in reverse, dragging an object from a notebook page into another application.

Hyperlinks and shortcuts to other files or to webpages can be inserted on a note-book page. This enables you to link quickly to other resources without having to open other applications first, so maintaining pace. To link to another file on your computer, tap the Attachments folder at the bottom of the right-hand side of the notebook page, or go to View>Attachments or use the keyboard shortcut Alt 3. This will bring up the Attachments view. To insert a shortcut to the file you want, tap on the Attach file shortcut icon on the toolbar, which looks like a paper clip with an arrow on it (it is ringed in red in Figure 6.5), or go to Insert>Shortcut to file. This will open a window in which you can select the file you want.

Tap on Open to attach the file to the notebook page. You will see that the number beside the Attachments folder on the right of the notebook page changes to a 1. When you are using the notebook, tapping on the Attachments folder will bring up the Attachments page, and you can then tap on the name of the file you want to open. To return to the notebook, tap on the icon for the notebook on the bottom

Figure 6.5 Attaching a shortcut to another document

toolbar, then go to View>Whiteboard or use Alt 1 on the keyboard to return to the Whiteboard view.

To link to a webpage, go into Attachments view (tap the Attachments folder on the bottom right of the notebook page, or go to View>Attachments, or use the keyboard shortcut Alt 3). Then tap on Insert>Hyperlink. This will bring up a box in which the URL of the webpage should be inserted. It is best to copy and paste this, to make sure there are no errors in it. The wording actually displayed on the notebook page can be changed, by tapping on the URL on the page and changing it to a title instead. Tapping on the shortcut arrow (a hand should appear if the hyperlink is active) will then allow the URL to be accessed.

The **Format menu** contains options for formatting text and for changing the thickness and colour of drawing objects. Background colour enables you to set the colour you want for your page – white may not always be best. White may reflect sunlight or other light in the room, so that some children cannot see what is on the board. A dark colour with a light-coloured font may be preferable. If you have children who have some form of dyslexia, again a different colour combination may suit them better.

Once you have set up a page, if you want to be sure that text is not inadvertently moved, use Format>Lock Position. The other option on the Format menu you may wish to explore is Transparency. To use this, select a picture or clip-art drawing. Format>Transparency gives you various degrees of transparency, so that you can reveal objects lying underneath each other.

The **Draw menu** includes lines, rectangles, ellipses, and so on. If you have the more complex toolbar open, many of the options on this menu will be displayed as icons. This menu also allows objects to be grouped together or ordered. Grouped objects can be resized or moved as a single object. Order allows you to decide which objects should be on top and which should be underneath, as well as enabling you to put certain objects into the background.

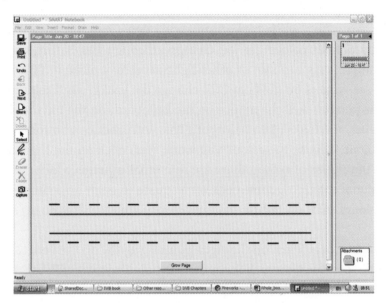

Figure 6.6 A page template for handwriting activities

Figure 6.6 shows a handwriting template on a coloured background, which was produced using the Draw menu. Initially, the handwriting template in the SMARTboard files was used as a guide, to keep the lines horizontal. The line tool (Draw>Line) was used to make one long line, and one very short line. The long line was copied (select, Ctrl C) and pasted (Ctrl V) onto the page to make the second long line. The short line was then copied several times to produce the dashed line. This line was selected, then grouped together as a single object (Ctrl G or Draw>Group), then copied and a second dashed line pasted onto the page. The four lines were placed using the guide lines, and grouped together.

At this point the group of lines was cut from the page (Ctrl X) and pasted onto a new page, with a plain coloured background (Format>Background colour). The lines were then made part of the background, so that they cannot be deleted or moved accidentally, using Draw>Order>Make background or Ctrl M. This is not irreversible; the lines can be taken out of the background using Draw>Order> Retrieve background or Ctrl K. Finally the page was saved with the other templates for use in several different resources.

Last, but not least, is the **Help menu.** Help menus can be a mixed blessing – you have to know what the item you want is called. However, looking through the Index can be a way round this problem. You can use the more specific options to remind yourself how to do a particular operation, or use the tutorial and the overviews to find out more about what your software can do. The more you use the Help menu when you are stuck, or have a question, the more familiar with its contents you will become.

ACTIVprimary flipchart

Getting started

A new flipchart with a white background will open when the software is opened, although the default colour can be changed through the Settings options (see below). White reflects sunlight or other lights, and may make it difficult for some children to see what is on the board. To change the background colour on a single page, tap the pen (or click the mouse on the keyboard) on the Fill tool (it is on the vertical toolbar, and looks like a paintpot). This will produce a bottom toolbar, with circles of colour. Choose the colour you want, then click on the flipchart page. In addition to the circles of colour, there are four small squares which can be used to select additional colours. Double click on a square to open up a choice of colours; for more colours, click on Define custom colours, which will open up a full colour spectrum.

To open a new page, click on the right-pointing arrow on the vertical toolbar; to go back to the previous page, click on the left-pointing arrow. To see all the pages in the current flipchart, click on the page number on the vertical toolbar. The pages will appear in a bottom horizontal toolbar. Any page can be accessed by clicking on it in this toolbar. To sort, copy or delete pages, you will need to be in Design Mode (see below). Click on the page sorter icon at the right of the bottom toolbar. This will take you into page sorter view, where various operations can be carried out on pages. Clicking on the smiley face will accept any changes, and return you to the normal flipchart view.

ACTIVprimary can be used without a board attached for preparation of resources, although a watermark will show across all flipchart pages, but this will not show when a board is attached. Some tools, such as the handwriting recognition tool and the fraction notation tool, will not work without a board, but all the other tools can be used so that full preparation can be done away from the board.

The annotation tools

If you open the ACTIVprimary software, then open a Word or PowerPoint document, or any other application, you will see a floating toolbar containing annotation tools which can be used over any application, including internet sites. This toolbar can be moved by dragging so that it is not in the way. The annotation tools include a pen, a highlighter, the Snapshot tool, and the clear screen tool. (When the next version of ACTIVprimary is released, there will be extra tools, such as Undo).

To start annotating, click on the tool you wish to use. While the annotation tools are active, the document being annotated is not active, and *vice versa*. For example, if the annotation tools are used to edit a passage in Word, while the tools are being used Word is inactive. To stop annotating, and return to the other document, use the Clear Screen icon on the floating toolbar. This will make the annotation layer disappear, and the other document will become active again.

At the moment, there is no direct way to save annotations on a document other than a flipchart, although this is to be part of the forthcoming update of the software. Perhaps the easiest way to keep annotations in the current version of the software is to use the Snapshot tool to 'photograph' either just the annotations, or the page with the annotations. This can be copied to the clipboard to paste into the document, or it can be copied directly into a flipchart (see how to use the Snapshot tool below). The annotations will no longer be live, but at least they can be saved. Photographing the annotations will remove them from the document, although they can be pasted back from the clipboard.

Teacher Tools

Unlike most other software, ACTIVprimary does not have a toolbar along the top allowing access to common menus. Instead it has a vertical toolbar (which can be positioned on the left or the right, see below) with icons giving access to various resources. Common operations, like saving and printing, are in the Teacher Tools. These are accessed by clicking on the top left-hand icon on the vertical toolbar, the 'Promethean man', and will appear as a horizontal row of icons. Figure 6.7 shows the Teacher Tools.

Figure 6.7 Teacher Tools

The first icon on the left on the horizontal Teacher toolbar opens a new flipchart, and the second opens an existing flipchart; the third and fourth icons are for saving and printing. The next icon resets a page, which returns a page to the last saved version if it has been annotated since saving. The fourth icon from the right gives teachers the option of writing notes to accompany a flipchart; this is very useful when resources are saved on a school network, so that teachers' notes can be kept with a flipchart. The third icon from the right takes you back to your computer desktop, and is the way to go to another application without actually closing ACTIVprimary. The second icon from the right is red in Figure 6.7, indicating that the flipchart is currently in Design Mode. Clicking it again switches it back to Presentation Mode, and is indicated by a yellow Promethean man.

The yellow icon with three dots gives a drop-down Menu. There are several choices here, of which Settings and Help are probably the most important initially. Settings gives various options, among them the choice of default colour for a flipchart and whether the vertical toolbar is on the right or the left. The vertical toolbar can be moved up and down by dragging. Help menus can be a mixed blessing – you have to know what the item you want is called. However, looking through the Index can be a way round this problem. These more specific options can be helpful in reminding you how to do a particular operation. You can also use the tutorials and the overviews to find out more about what your software can do. The more you use the Help menu when you are stuck or have a question, the more familiar with its contents you will become.

Presentation and Design Mode

When a flipchart is opened it will be in Presentation Mode, which is indicated by the yellow border around the Promethean man on the vertical toolbar and in the Teacher Tools. As its name suggests, Presentation Mode is meant to be used when a flipchart is used for a presentation in the classroom. In this mode, objects on a page can be moved by dragging them, and can be resized. Double clicking or right clicking on an object will bring up a floating toolbar, as in Figure 6.8, which allows an object to be made larger (+ icon), smaller (− icon), deleted (dustbin icon) or duplicated (double page icon).

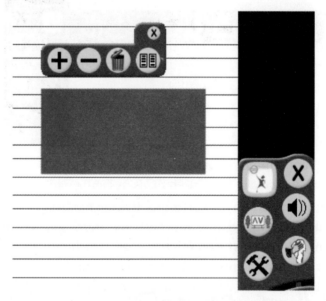

Figure 6.8 Icons for changing an object in Presentation Mode

Almost everything other than annotating a page or moving objects on it will need to be done in Design Mode. For instance, the order in which objects appear on the page can be organised by going into Design Mode, then right clicking on the objects. There are three layers, top, middle and bottom, and a choice of front or back on each layer. By default, inserted backgrounds will be put on the bottom layer, inserted images and text on the middle layer, and annotations on the top layer. To find out which layer an object or annotation is on, click on the object or annotation, bringing up the floating toolbar. Choosing the far right icon, Object properties, will cause a box to appear. This box will indicate which layer an object is in, and gives options which enable that layer to be changed. Whether the object is to the front or the back of the layer can also be changed. Other options enable objects to give a page change or to play a sound when they are clicked.

Writing and drawing freehand

To write or draw freehand, select the pencil icon on the vertical toolbar. This will bring up a range of pencil and highlighter widths and colours, and eraser widths at the bottom of the window. Simply choose your options, and start writing or drawing. The 'Draw point to point' icon at the right of the bottom toolbar means that you can use a pencil tool to draw straight lines which go from one point to another – click the pen or mouse to indicate where points are to be. Enclosed shapes created in this way can be filled with colour, using the Fill icon on the vertical toolbar.

To remove freehand writing or drawing, actions can be undone one at a time with the Undo icon, and can be put back with the Redo icon (these can both be found at the bottom of the vertical toolbar). Alternatively there are eraser tools, which can be found on the bottom toolbar with the pencil tools. These do not actually erase what is written, but put a layer over it so that it is no longer visible. This layer can be removed with the Undo tool or moved aside, showing the original writing or drawing still visible on the page. To erase freehand writing permanently, use the Eraser icon at the top of the vertical toolbar: this gives three options, of which the right-hand one, Erase all scribbles, will remove all freehand writing, highlighting and erasing.

ACTIVprimary includes a handwriting recognition tool, although this can only be used when the board is attached. To use this, click on the Special tools icon on the vertical toolbar (hammer and spanner), then select the 'ab' tool. This will bring up a dialogue box which can be written in, as in Figure 6.9.

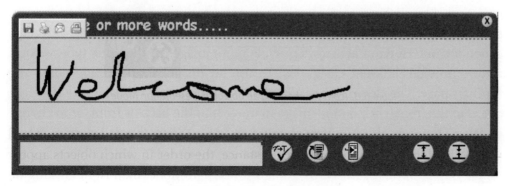

Figure 6.9 Handwriting recognition

The software will attempt to recognise what is written. If you are happy with what it produces, then accept the text, and close the box. If not, there are options to edit or redo the text. The text can also be edited as text in the flipchart, if the recogniser has difficulty with a particular word.

The dialogue box also provides adjustable guidelines for children learning to write. They can write into the box, using the lines as guides, and then the resulting text conversion can be used as an indication of how well their handwriting is progressing, and saved for future comparisons, or for report writing.

Inserting typed text

To insert typed text, click on the T icon on the vertical toolbar. The bottom toolbar will show a range of options, including font type, size and colour. Once these have been chosen, just start typing on the flipchart page. When you have finished, click on the selector arrow (the large black diagonal arrow on the vertical toolbar). The text can then be moved by dragging it. It can be edited by double clicking or right clicking on it to bring up the floating toolbar, then choosing the T icon. Insert the cursor where you want to edit and add something else, or select what is wrong and over-type. To remove typed text, double click or right click on the text, and click on the dustbin icon to remove the text. Alternatively, you can remove all objects on the page, by using the Erase icon at the top of the vertical toolbar – the second option, Remove all objects, will remove text.

The keyboard icon on the right of the Text toolbar at the bottom of the window brings up the onscreen keyboard. Right-clicking on this keyboard shows the four available options. The two versions of a child's keyboard have letters in alphabetical order, rather than in the usual 'qwerty' order. The two adult versions have the normal order of the letters. ACTIVprimary remembers the last version used, and opens this each time until it is altered.

Inserting pictures

Figure 6.10 shows a new page created with handwritten and typed text and an image put together from the ACTIVprimary resources. A wealth of resources can be accessed by clicking on the book icon at the bottom of the vertical toolbar (in red in Figure 6.10). Images will appear in the bottom toolbar, together with navigation arrows. Horizontal arrows provide more images of the same type, vertical arrows provide different categories. To use an image, simply drag it onto the flipchart page. The clown was made up of several images. To make sure the right one is to the front, click on the image to move it to the back or front, or to change its layer. There is also a rubber-stamp tool here. When this is selected, it will produce further copies of the chosen item.

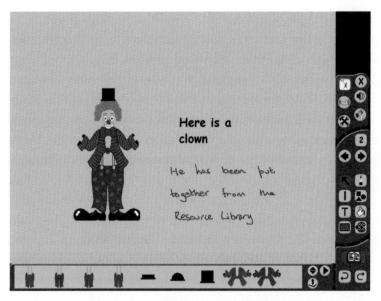

Figure 6.10 Inserting pictures in ACTIVprimary

Backgrounds

The Grid icon towards the bottom left of the vertical toolbar opens up a menu of grids, squared background, dots, and so on, at the bottom of the screen. This toolbar also allows you to change the colour of many of the grids, scale them up or down, hide them, and make them 'snapto' (so that lines or points near the intersections of grid lines automatically snap to the intersections). Choose your options, and then drag the grid onto the screen. The Background icon, next to the Grid icon, opens up a range of different backgrounds to use. These include lined paper, maps, mazes, board games, and many others. Grids can be put above other backgrounds if desired.

You can also make your own backgrounds to save and use in future flipcharts. When you have designed your background, just right click on the page. You may find that either Add grid to library or Add background to library is highlighted, and clicking on this will allow you to save a grid or background for future use. If not, use the camera tool to make an image of your background (this should be the whole screen, although not the toolbars). Open the Background toolbar, and then drag your image onto this toolbar. A pop-up menu will ask you to name it, and it will then be saved for future use.

Special Tools

An extremely useful icon is the Special Tools icon. This is the second icon down from the Promethean man on the left of the vertical toolbar, and looks like a crossed hammer and spanner. Clicking on this provides a range of special tools along the bottom of the screen. Some of these tools are technical tools, such as the

Snapshot tool which allows you to 'photograph' anything on your screen, in both ACTIVprimary software and any other application, including the internet. Other tools are pedagogical, such as the protractor and the dice.

On the extreme left is the Spotlight icon. There are four different versions of the spotlight to choose. This enables you to show part of your screen, while hiding the rest. Next is the Reveal icon, which provides a screen across the Window. This screen can be lowered from the top, to reveal gradually the content of a page, as you might move a piece of paper down an overhead projector transparency.

Next are the pedagogical tools. The third icon is the dice tool. Clicking on this gives a pop-up menu, which has options for choosing how many dice are rolled, rolling the dice, and finding the total on the faces of the dice. The fourth tool is a protractor, and there are 360 degree and 180 degree versions. Figure 6.11 shows the 360 degree protractor centred on the intersection of two lines, and rotated so that the 0/360 degree line is on the right-hand line. This tool can be moved and rotated even if the flipchart is not in Design view, so that children can use it to practise measuring angles.

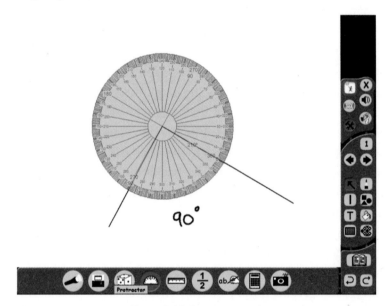

Figure 6.11 Protractor tool

Next is a ruler with two versions, either centimetres (15 cm) or inches (12 inches). Like the protractors, these can be moved and rotated in Presentation mode.

Fourth from the right is a fraction tool, which gives fractions in correct notation, and third from the right is the handwriting recognition tool, which was described above. These two are not enabled unless the board is attached. Last but one on the right is a calculator, which comes in child and adult versions. Unfortunately, this is a simple calculator, which requires the user to know the order of operations, which is not ideal for primary age children. For example, if the calculation $2 + 3 \times 6$ is keyed into the calculator, it gives the answer 30 which is incorrect (3×6 should be calculated first, regardless of the order in which the operations are written, so the correct answer is 20 – this issue will be addressed in the next version of ACTIVprimary). More usefully, this tool can be used over other applications, not just when a flipchart is being used.

The final icon on this toolbar is the Snapshot tool, which is another technical tool, and is also on the floating tools which can be used to annotate anything on the whiteboard. This allows 'photos' to be taken of any image on the computer and then pasted into any application. There are three ways of defining the area to be photographed, and there are also options of pasting it directly into either the current page in a flipchart, a new page in a flipchart, or to the Windows clipboard (from which it is accessible from any application). To copy an image to the clipboard, right-click on the area to be copied and choose Snap to clipboard. To paste into another application, use copy and paste.

Incorporating sounds

At the moment, sounds are the only external files which can be attached to a flipchart, and this is covered in detail in Chapter 7. There are also a large number of different sounds available in the Resource Book, including alphabet sounds, clapping, music, seaside sounds and many others. Click on the book icon at the bottom of the vertical toolbar, and navigate until you find the folder of sounds. To use one of these, just drag it onto your flipchart page, and position it where you want it. To operate it, click on it. The Sound Controller, at the top of the vertical toolbar, gives various options for operating sounds, including stopping them.

PowerPoint or IWB software?

Presentations can be created in both PowerPoint and IWB software. If you only have a data projector, then you have no choice about which to use. However, if you have an IWB, then you may wonder which is better.

This depends on how you wish to use your presentation and what content you wish to incorporate. If you wish to produce a really professional-looking presentation, with no toolbars around the outside of the slides, then PowerPoint is better. If you want to animate your presentation, again PowerPoint does this really well. If you might want to annotate pages, but will not want to keep the annotations, then again you might choose to use PowerPoint.

However, if you want to be able to annotate pages as you go, and keep the annotated pages for future use, it is better to use IWB software. You will also have a greater range of resources you can incorporate, such as page templates or backgrounds with IWB software. Moving objects or rotating them during a presentation is easy to do in IWB software. It can be done in PowerPoint but would have to be decided during preparation, so IWB software allows a much more dynamic presentation where complete spontaneity is possible.

It is possible to do nearly everything you can do in PowerPoint in IWB software, and *vice versa*. Some things are more easily achieved in one type of software than the other, but this depends to an extent on what type of IWB software you have. Experimentation will be necessary to explore what your IWB software will do, and whether it is easier to achieve a given effect with that or with PowerPoint.

PART 3

Lesson Resources

In this section, lesson resources which can be used with an IWB are discussed. Instructions are given for all resources, where these have not already been covered in Part 2. Many of the resources do not involve specific IWB software, so teachers with different types of boards should still find much that is useful here, and can also be used by teachers using data projectors without an IWB. Even the resources created for use with ACTIVprimary or SMARTboard software can be used by those with different types of IWB software if they use their own board's User Guide to help them create similar resources of their own. All instructions should be used in conjunction with those in the previous chapters where necessary.

Resources are grouped into chapters for English, Mathematics and other curriculum areas, which include Science, Geography, History, Personal, Social and Health Education and Citizenship. However, many of the ideas discussed can be used in curriculum areas other than those for which they are presented here. In each chapter, resources are given which use generic software (such as Word), presentations (which use PowerPoint and/or IWB software) and, in some cases, use of the internet and additional ICT. Other forms of software are not covered. Once a teacher knows how to use an IWB with, say, Word or PowerPoint, then using any other software available should not be a problem.

Pictures of the resources described are included, together with annotation where appropriate. Although these show ACTIVprimary or SMARTboard tools, any IWB tools can be used. The pictures should not be taken to imply that a resource can only be used in a certain type of software, or with one particular set of annotation tools.

All the resources described here are available on the accompanying CD, and can be edited so that they suit the requirements of a particular class. Suggestions on how to do this or additional technical details not covered in Part 2 are added in separate boxes.

The ideas covered are not meant to be in any way exhaustive, merely to suggest to beginners ways of using the IWB, and to present more techniques to those who wish to extend what they are doing at present. Some are very simple, and take very little time to edit or to produce similar resources. Others are more complicated, requiring greater technical knowledge. My hope is that teachers will use these ideas to get them started on using their own IWB, and that they will use them as a starting point for their own journey of discovery.

CHAPTER 7

English

Many resources for the literacy hour can be prepared with a minimum of preparation, saved, changed, and used again. This means teachers and schools can quickly build up a bank of resources for use both with a whole class or for small groups. Worksheets can be displayed on the IWB for whole class discussion to make sure everyone knows what they should be doing. They can also be printed out for children to use in subsequent individual activities, so that all resources and worksheets are customised for the needs of the class.

Examples given in this chapter include using Word, presentations (both PowerPoint and IWB software), attaching sounds to a presentation, and using additional ICT, such as digital photos or videos.

Word documents

Word documents can be used in a variety of ways with an IWB to enhance the literacy hour. The examples given here can be used to help children with punctuation, proof reading and editing, and can also be used as starting points for various types of writing. Many of these activities make use of the floating tools for annotation of a document. Initial class discussion, focused on a document on the IWB, could then be followed with individual activity in which children write freehand or at the computer their own versions of what has been done.

Punctuation and imaginative writing

- Word document

- available on accompanying CD, *Punctuation.doc*

- can be edited for use by children learning about punctuation, and also as a starting point for imaginative writing of their own.

Punctuation.doc contains a piece of text requiring punctuation. This can be done as a whole class activity initially, so that the children can discuss together how they think the passage should be punctuated. The whiteboard annotation tools provide an easy way to add the punctuation the children suggest. Using a different colour means that additions show up clearly, as in Figure 7.1.

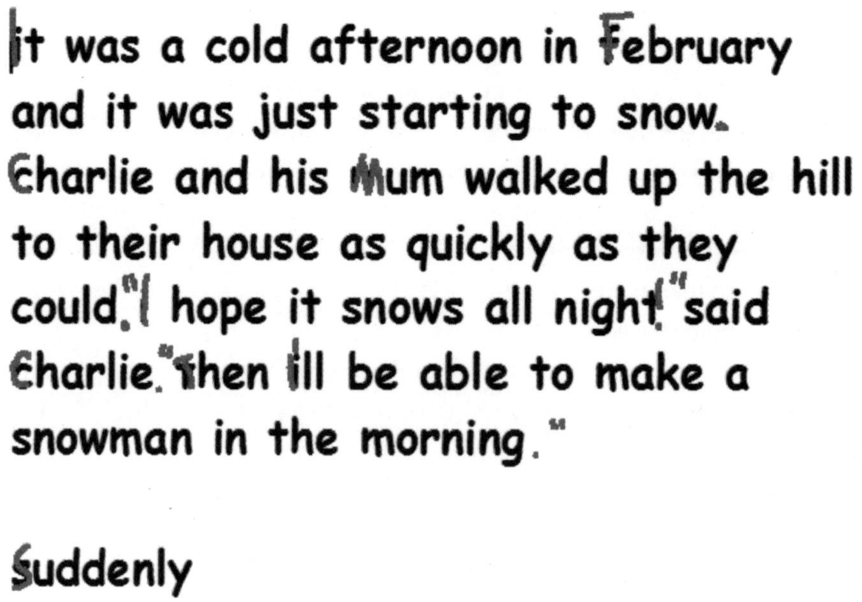

> It was a cold afternoon in February and it was just starting to snow. Charlie and his Mum walked up the hill to their house as quickly as they could."I hope it snows all night "said Charlie. Then Ill be able to make a snowman in the morning."
>
> ## Suddenly

Figure 7.1 Simple punctuation exercise using annotation tools

Once punctuation has been suggested, it can be added to the original document, which can then be printed out for the children to continue the story in their own way. Changing the text allows this exercise to be used again and again, and by almost any age group.

Muddled punctuation

- Word document
- available on accompanying CD, *Muddled_punctuation.doc*
- can be edited for children learning about punctuation.

"i wish I could go to the ball, like my ugly
sisters!? said Cinderella miserably. I never
have any fun.! ?you shall go to the ball,, said
someone from behind her. .what. who was
that,, said cinderella. Startled; it was her
fairy godmother who had appeared behind
her: Waving a magic wand? i need you to go
and get me a few things' a pumpkin and four
white mice should do? with a wave of her

Figure 7.2 Muddled punctuation

Like the previous example, this is just a piece of text, typed out in Word. However, capital letters have been removed from where they are needed, and put in elsewhere, and all the punctuation has been randomly changed. Figure 7.2 shows how it might be started as a whole class activity or perhaps as a small group activity, using the annotation pen. Activities of this sort are ideal for initiating class discussion on the role of punctuation, and what specific punctuation marks are needed in a given situation. Again, it can easily be edited to suit particular teaching objectives.

Coded punctuation

- Word document

- available on accompanying CD, *Coded_punctuation.doc*

- can be edited for all children learning about punctuation.

Can you imagine what it would be like if you could not just turn a tap on whenever you wanted a drink of water⬚ ⬚people don❼t always have access to clean water in many parts of the world⬚ in Bangladesh⬚ in Albania⬚ in Malawi and Liberia⬚ many people still have to walk huge distances to collect water⬚ bringing back to their homes in jars carried on their heads⬚ we❼re used to getting clean water⬚ but they have to put up with whatever they can find⬚ if people don❼t have clean water⬚ they become ill⬚ and can❼t look after their crops properly⬚

Figure 7.3 Coded punctuation

This passage has all its punctuation replaced by a code which has to be cracked. Capital letters also have to be inserted in the right places. An issue this raises is why there is a wiggly red line underneath one of the words, leading to discussion about spell-checking and grammar-checking. This could be started as a whole class activity using the annotation pens, with children continuing on their own using worksheets printed out from the Word document. Similar exercises can easily be produced, by typing out a piece of text, and replacing all the punctuation with symbols.

Producing a simple code

This code was produced by typing the correct symbols in a Wingdings font. Word contains several fonts which use symbols rather than the normal letters and punctuation marks, and any of these can be used to create a simple code. This has the advantage that the code can be checked by reverting from the symbol font to a normal font.

Boring sentences

- Word document
- available on accompanying CD, *Boring_sentences.doc*
- can be edited for all children who are writing in sentences.

Figure 7.4 shows how this document might be used. The boring sentences on the left have been changed to more interesting ones on the right. In these, adjectives have been highlighted in yellow, adverbs in green, and an adjectival phrase in blue. The class could do one or two examples all together, leading into discussion of what makes writing interesting, or alternatively to the role of adverbs and adjectives in sentences. This type of activity could also be used to introduce new vocabulary. Children could then continue by themselves from a worksheet, printed out from the Word file, perhaps typing their own interesting sentences onto another page for later discussion all together. The resource given can easily be edited to suit the age of the children, and the specific objectives of the lesson.

Boring sentences

1. Sunlight came through the window.

2. The piano was kept in the parlour.

3. The tower is made of brick.

4. The boat came round a bend in the river.

5. A windmill could be seen on the horizon.

Interesting sentences

1. Bright sunlight came through the square window.

2. The tall, black piano was kept in the dim, cool parlour.

3. The tall, red tower is made of crumbling brick.

4. The dark green boat came slowly round a slight bend in the muddy river.

5. A black windmill with white sails could be seen low on the horizon.

Figure 7.4 Making boring sentences more interesting

Producing columns in Word

Format>Columns is used in the Word document to divide the page into two columns, so that the 'boring' sentences can be put down the left-hand side of the page, and the interesting versions down the right-hand side. The left-hand column needs to be typed first, then the right-hand column. Note that the file is shown in Full Screen View (View>Full Screen), as this removes the toolbars, and means that more of the screen is visible without the need to scroll up and down.

Proof reading and editing a narrative

- Word document

- available on accompanying CD, *Edit.doc*

- can be substituted by any piece of writing which needs to be edited or redrafted.

This document was written by James (aged 8), and is a first draft of a piece about himself. It is an interesting, lively piece of writing, which tells us a lot about James, but it could do with a little more work to produce a polished piece. The purpose of this activity is to enable the class to see that editing and redrafting are necessary activities, and to give the teacher the opportunity to model how this might be done.

The focus could be on technical aspects, such as spelling, sentence and paragraph construction, or it could be on developing the content of the piece. In Figure 7.5, the IWB annotation tools have been used to comment and indicate where editing is necessary.

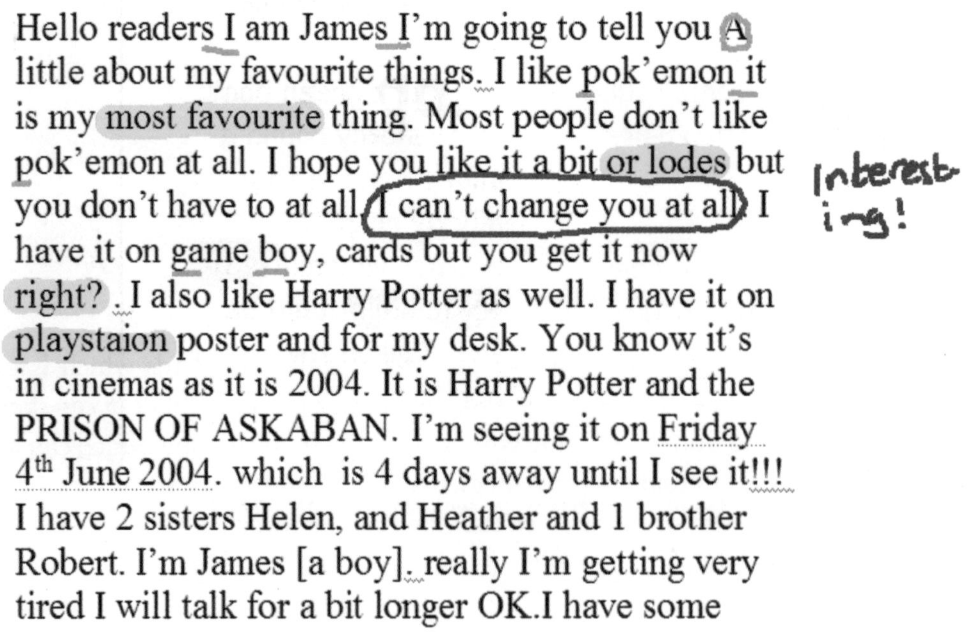

Hello readers I am James I'm going to tell you A little about my favourite things. I like pok'emon it is my most favourite thing. Most people don't like pok'emon at all. I hope you like it a bit or lodes but you don't have to at all. I can't change you at all I have it on game boy, cards but you get it now right? . I also like Harry Potter as well. I have it on playstaion poster and for my desk. You know it's in cinemas as it is 2004. It is Harry Potter and the PRISON OF ASKABAN. I'm seeing it on Friday 4th June 2004. which is 4 days away until I see it!!! I have 2 sisters Helen, and Heather and 1 brother Robert. I'm James [a boy]. really I'm getting very tired I will talk for a bit longer OK.I have some

Interesting!

Figure 7.5 Editing a text

After starting this as a whole class activity, children could then go on to correct it themselves, or work on a draft of their own. Editing could be done at the computer or freehand, perhaps using a different colour to show changes.

Using presentations

Word cards 1

- IWB software
- available on accompanying CD, *Word_cards1.xbk* or *Word_cards1.flp*.
- can be edited for children learning to recognise words.

IWB software can be used to prepare varied and colourful word cards for children learning word recognition. In Figure 7.6, the notebook page starts with just the apple showing. When asked what it is, the children will respond that it is an apple. One of them can then come up to the board and use the eraser to find the hidden word.

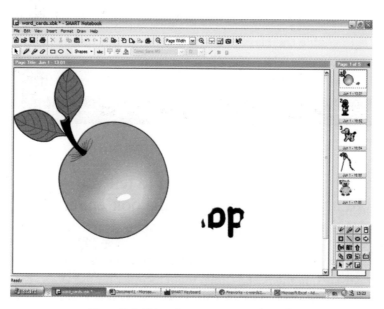

Figure 7.6 Using the eraser to reveal words

The pages in this resource show images accompanied by words which have been covered using a pen of the same colour as the background. Children can then use the eraser tool to find the missing words. It is a useful technique, which can be used in a variety of different circumstances, to use a layer of colour the same as the background to hide text or pictures, so that they can be revealed in due course.

Word cards 2

- IWB software
- available on accompanying CD, *Word_cards2.xbk* or *Word_cards2.flp*
- can be edited for use by children learning to recognise and copy words.

This resource contains pictures of words for children to recognise and copy, which can be used to supplement work with objects. The large IWB display is much easier for children to see than pictures held up by the teacher, and there is the additional advantage that children can write on the board for themselves.

Figure 7.7 Copying words

Creating a page template with handwriting lines (SMARTboard)

On a fresh page start by drawing lines at the required spacings. A grid or lined background may help with this. Choose the background colour you want. Then select all the lines, right-click on them, and Group them together (or use Draw>Group). Move the lines to the place on the page you want them, and resize them as required. When you are happy with the layout of the page, go to File>Save page as template. A box will open, allowing you to name the page and save it in the folder you want. This will save the whole page as a basic template for future use.

Creating a page background with handwriting lines (ACTIVprimary)

Go to a fresh page in Design mode, and draw the lines you want at the required spacing – a grid background may help with this. Straight lines can be drawn with the pencil tool and Draw point-to-point. Also selecting snap-to-grid helps with this. Then, choose the background colour you want. Once the template is finished, use the Snapshot tool (found in the Special tools, hammer and spanner icon on the vertical toolbar) to photograph the page. Open the Backgrounds toolbar, choosing the folder you want this background to go into. Now drag your page onto the toolbar. This page will then be available for use as a background whenever you want.

Forming simple sentences

- IWB software

- available on accompanying CD, *Simple_sentences.flp* or *Simple_sentences.xbk*

- can be edited for children beginning to write in sentences.

Figure 7.8 shows a page from this resource. There is a simple scene for the class to discuss and then formulate a sentence describing it. A child could then perhaps come out and write a sentence on the handwriting lines, or the teacher could write the sentence for the children to read. If children fill in the sentences, the pages could be saved or printed out for a portfolio of their work for Parents Night, or to help with recording progress.

Figure 7.8 Writing simple sentences

Negatives

- IWB software
- available on accompanying CD, *Negatives.flp* or *Negatives.xbk*
- can be edited for children writing in simple sentences.

There are five pages in this resource. Each shows a picture and a piece of text, which says the opposite to what the picture shows, as in Figure 7.9. There are handwriting lines for children to write the correct sentence, which is the negative of the sentence shown. Again, examples of children's handwriting could be kept for future use.

Figure 7.9 Introducing negatives

Class dictionary

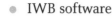

- IWB software

- exemplar page available on accompanying CD, *Dictionary.xbk* or *Dictionary.flp*

- cumulative resource, suitable for children building up their vocabulary.

As children increase their vocabularies, they can start to develop a class dictionary which will also be helpful for spellings they find difficult. This is a cumulative resource which can be built up over a long period of time. Each letter of the alphabet can be given as many pages as required, because pages can always be inserted. The resource provided is an example of a page, rather than a complete resource. This page can be edited to provide the start of a class's own dictionary. An example of a page is shown in Figure 7.10.

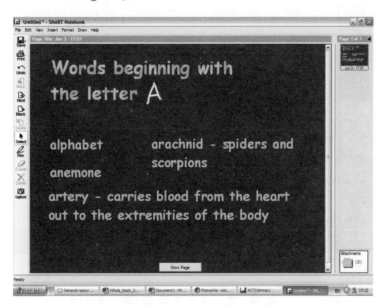

Figure 7.10 Example of a class dictionary

Perhaps children could take it in turns to maintain the class dictionary for a day, being responsible for adding new words, spellings and definitions, as needed. The dictionary could be displayed on the IWB for easy reference when children are writing anything where its use could be helpful.

Verb tenses

- IWB software

- available on accompanying CD, *Past_tenses.xbk* or *Past_tenses.flp*

- can be edited for use with children learning about verb tenses.

This resource contains a single page, with four examples. Figure 7.11 shows some of the ways the examples might be completed, using the pen annotation tool. Pages can be printed out for children to do as an individual activity after whole class discussion of ways of forming past tenses. This could be changed to include only verbs which form the past tense by adding *–ed*, or it could be used as an opportunity to discuss verbs which do not. It could also be used to stimulate discussion of the nuances different versions of the past tense give to the English language. Equally, it could be edited for learning about present or future tenses.

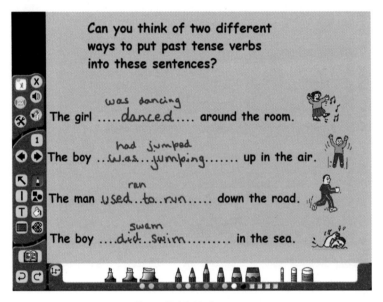

Figure 7.11 Verb tenses

Spelling words beginning with 'c'

- IWB software

- available on accompanying CD, *c-words.xbk* or *c-words.flp*

- can be edited to use with children having problems spelling words beginning with a particular letter.

Figure 7.12 shows an activity to help with the spelling of words beginning with the letter 'c'. The purpose of this resource is to help children see the variety of words which begin with the letter 'c', and how pronunciation and spelling relate to each other. It could be used as a whole class activity to start a lesson, with children discussing what the words might be, and how to spell them. A printed version could then be used for follow-up work.

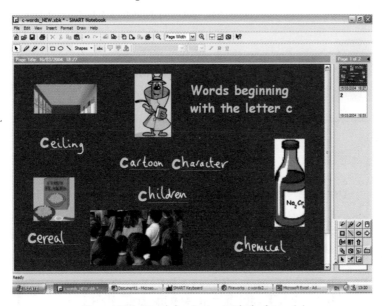

Figure 7.12 Words beginning with the letter 'c'

Stimulus for creative writing or drama

- PowerPoint document

- available on accompanying CD, *Dear_diary.ppt*

- can be edited for most age groups.

In this resource, a series of PowerPoint slides are used to give a basic story on which any kind of writing could be based. It could also be used as a stimulus for drama or for discussion of issues in PSHE or Citizenship. Similar resources could be produced using slides containing text, bullet points, questions, pictures, a sound narrative or conversation, or video clips.

The example given on the CD, *Dear_diary.ppt*, consists of diary entries by a fictitious girl from the mid-twentieth century for the first couple of weeks of the new school year. A sample page is shown in Figure 7.13. This resource could be used in its present form to explore issues such as bullying or taking responsibility for your own actions, as well as more mundane aspects of the beginning of a new year. Equally it could be used to discuss diaries, what their purpose is, who might keep one, famous diaries, and so on.

Figure 7.13 Diary entry

This resource could be used in a number of ways as a stimulus for creative writing. Children could write an account of the two weeks from the perspective of one of the characters mentioned, or they could continue doing the diary entries for the next few days. Alternatively, it could be a stimulus for a dramatic recreation of the marble incident, allowing children to discuss how the situation would have appeared to the various participants.

This particular resource was created in PowerPoint, so teachers using data projectors rather than IWBs can also use it, but it could have been created just as easily using IWB software.

Writing a biography

- IWB software

- available on accompanying CD, *Biography.flp* or *Biography.xbk*

- can be edited for children to write a biography of an imaginary or real person.

A presentation (whether in PowerPoint or in IWB software) can be used as a starting point for children to write a biography. Images or a recording or someone's reminiscences could be used to stimulate children's imaginations. The advantage of using IWB software here, rather than PowerPoint, is that the images can be annotated as the class discusses the story, and then saved for use on another occasion, if required. Of course, PowerPoint can also be annotated, but saving the annotations with the original file will depend on what type of IWB software is available.

The IWB files prepared for the CD only contain a picture of two houses and some questions. Almost anything could be used to stimulate discussion of people's lives, what is interesting about them, and what kind of material might be used in a biography. The purpose of this picture and the accompanying questions is to stimulate class discussion, which can be recorded in the IWB file, and then used by the children to help them write their biographies, as in Figure 7.14.

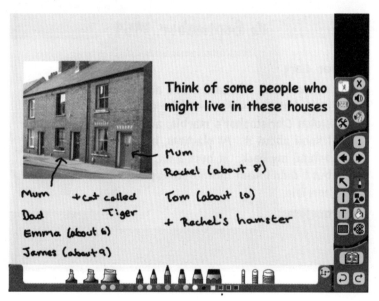

Figure 7.14 Stimulus for biographical writing

Using an IWB for this means that the main points of the discussion can be recorded, which might include a review of what a biography is, or the main points of the stories of the people who live in the houses. This can then be saved for reference if the activity takes more than one session, or if the teacher feels it could usefully be revisited on another occasion.

Displaying children's work

Invitations to the ball

- IWB software together with scanner

- example available on accompanying CD, *Invitations.xbk* or *Invitations.flp*

- can be edited for use in displaying children's work.

If a school has a scanner then children's work can be displayed for the whole class to see, either as a celebration of the work or for discussion. In Figure 7.15, there are three examples of invitations children aged 6 to 7 did. They had been using the story of Cinderella as a resource for a number of different activities, which included sending each other invitations to a ball or a party. Showing everyone's invitations on the IWB has much more impact than holding them up at the front of the room, and there is tremendous scope for using a scanner together with an IWB to display children's work in this way. PowerPoint could be used for this purpose as well.

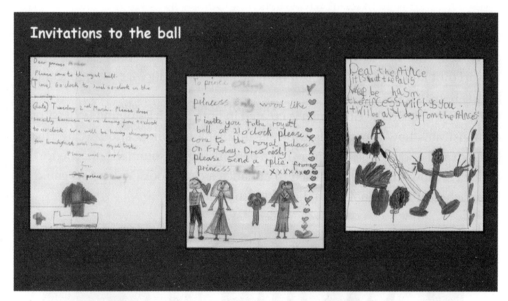

Figure 7.15 Invitations to the ball – celebrating children's work

---

Using scanned work in a SMARTboard notebook

A picture can be inserted directly into a notebook from a scanner. Once the picture has been put into the scanner, go to Insert>Picture from scanner. Alternatively, scanning a piece of work into the computer will produce a picture file. Click on this to select it and press Ctrl C to copy it, or use Edit>Copy. Now go to your notebook. Ctrl V, or Edit>Paste can be used to paste the picture onto the notebook page. You can then resize it or move it as necessary.

Using scanned work in an ACTIVboard flipchart

Scan the work into the computer to produce a picture file. Click on this to select it and press Ctrl C to copy it. Now go to your flipchart, making sure you are in Design Mode. Right click on the page, and choose Paste image from clipboard from the menu. This will paste the picture onto the flipchart page. You can then resize it or move it as necessary.

Including sound/video files

Class book

- PowerPoint or IWB software plus attached sound file

- exemplar available on accompanying CD, *Class_book.ppt*, *Class_book.xbk*, or *Class_book.flp*

- can be edited for children of any age to make their own class book or a document to celebrate a particular event or visit.

The IWB can be used to make and present resources that really belong to the class. Groups of children can take it in turns to create their own pages, using their own drawings, text or written material and accompanying voice-over or video. PowerPoint and IWB software can both be used to produce a class book, and this idea is revisited in Chapter 9.

The example on the CD, which is created in both PowerPoint and IWB software, demonstrates how a page might be set up using drawings and text by Heather (aged 6) and a sound file. The page has a demonstration sound file attached, to give an idea of how this might be used to enhance a class book. Video files could also be attached, if the school has a digital video camera.

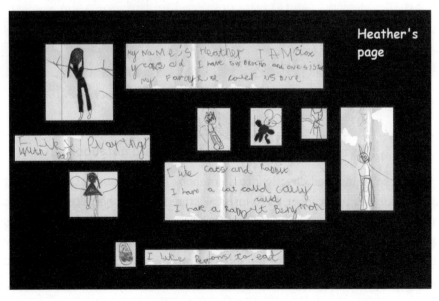

Figure 7.16 Heather's page

The pictures and text could be created directly on the IWB, or they could be scanned into the computer from work done on paper, as was done here. A dark-coloured background was used in this picture to give a contrast to Heather's drawings and what she has written about herself. If the work is scanned in from paper-based work, then in IWB software the Screen capture/Snapshot tool can be used to copy sections of the drawing and text so that it can be placed on the page as the child wants. Pasting images into IWB software from a scanner was described in the previous section.

Scanning the images

Initially, Heather did drawings and wrote about them, on a single sheet of A4 paper, telling us something about herself. When A4 pages are previewed in a scanner, there is an option to choose a small area of the page. In this way, small drawings or pieces of text can be made into separate images, as has been done here. Alternatively, the Screen Capture/Snapshot tool in IWB software can be used to 'photograph' sections of the page, and place the resulting images onto an IWB page.

Pasting the images into PowerPoint

There are two ways to do this. Images can be selected after scanning, then copied (Edit>Copy or Ctrl C) and pasted (Edit>Paste or Ctrl V) directly onto the PowerPoint slide. Alternatively, they can be inserted using Insert>Picture>From file.

Once the page is ready, a voice-over or video can be added of the child talking about what she has written, or suitable noises can be added to accompany pictures. A voice-over can be recorded directly using SMARTboard software or PowerPoint. Attaching a sound file can be also created outside of those applications, and then attached to the page/slide, and at present this is the only way to attach a sound file to an ACTIVprimary flipchart page (although this is due to change when the software is updated). If you have a digital video recorder, follow the instructions to create a video file, then attach it to the page in the same way as in the instructions below for a sound file (but note that at present, video files cannot be attached to ACTIVprimary flipchart pages).

Creating a sound file outside the IWB software or PowerPoint

You will need a computer with a sound card and a microphone. If your computer does not have an internal microphone, you will need to attach an external microphone. It is then straightforward to create a sound file in Windows XP. Go to the Start button and click on All programs>Accessories>Entertainment>Sound recorder. This will bring up the Sound recorder. All you then have to do is click on the button with a red dot to start the recording. Once the recording has been completed, it can be saved as a sound file.

To use this file in ACTIVprimary, it must be saved in c:\Documents and Settings\All users\Shared Documents\ACTIVsoftware\ACTIVprimary\Resources\Library (this is the file path for Windows XP; for other versions of Windows, go to www.promethean.co.uk/index.htm, then to Main Menu>ACTIVsoftware usergroup, where you will be asked to login, and then go to the ACTIVprimary area>Resources to find the appropriate filepath). Save the file in the Sounds folder.

It is as well to ensure before a child starts recording that everything is working correctly, as sometimes some of the volume settings on the computer may be set at mute, which may prevent the sound being recorded. Otherwise, if nothing seems to be happening, it could be that the microphone is faulty or in need of a new battery.

Creating a sound file on a SMARTboard

Tap the SMARTboard icon, and then select Recorder. This opens the Recorder toolbar. This gives you options to start and stop recording, and to pause the recording. The Options button enables you to choose the settings you want for sound quality.

Creating a sound file in PowerPoint

Go to Insert>Movies and sounds>Record sounds. This opens the Recorder toolbar. This gives you options to start and stop recording, and to pause the recording.

Attaching the sound file in PowerPoint

Select the image to which you want the sound file to be attached. Then either go to Insert>Hyperlink, or use Ctrl K on the keyboard. This will bring up a box, which gives you various options: Existing file or webpage allows you to choose the file you want.

Attaching the sound file in ACTIVprimary

Double click on the image to which you want to attach the sound file. On the toolbar which appears, click on the right hand icon, Object Properties, and a box will open. Towards the bottom of this, you will see Click Action. Select Play Sound from the box here. You will then see Select a Sound below – choose your file in the box underneath this.

Attaching the sound file on a SMARTboard

Tap on the Attachments button on the bottom right of the screen, or go to View>Attachments. Tapping on the paperclip icon on the toolbar opens up your files, and you can select your sound file.

Playing the sound file

In PowerPoint and ACTIVprimary, just tap or click on the image to which you have attached it. On a SMARTboard, tap on the attachment icon, and then on the name of the file. You can stop a sound file in PowerPoint by pressing 'esc' (Escape) on the keyboard. On the SMARTboard, press the Stop button in Windows Media Player. In ACTIVprimary, use the loudspeaker icon to the top right of the vertical toolbar. There are various options here to change the volume, stop the sound file, and so on.

CHAPTER 8

Mathematics

There are many resources available in IWB software, in other software available in primary schools and on the internet, which will make Maths lessons more interactive and more dynamic. Appendix 1 contains some suggestions for websites which may be useful.

The resources in this chapter use Excel spreadsheets, presentation software (PowerPoint and IWB software), and also discuss how a webpage can be adapted for whole class use.

Excel documents

There is a tendency for primary teachers to think that using spreadsheets is more appropriate for their secondary colleagues, but spreadsheets can be used to provide many activities which can be used in primary mathematics. The resources here use Excel's random number generator. Because these resources rely on random numbers, they can be used repeatedly, with a new set of questions for children to work on every time.

In this section, the boxes contain technical detail on how to use Excel to provide random numbers, and how to change the number ranges in the resources provided. These can safely be ignored on a first reading, but will help if later you want to edit the resources provided, or make similar ones of your own. We start with a brief explanation of how to get Excel to generate random numbers.

Producing random numbers in Excel

Excel recognises that it is being asked to work out a formula by an initial = sign. INT is used in the formula to take the integer (or whole number) part of the following number, and RAND asks Excel for a random number, which will be greater than or equal to 0 and less than 1.

To illustrate, suppose you want a random number between 0 and 9. The formula required is =INT(RAND()*10). Now let's suppose Excel provides the random number 0.92345. The *10 in the formula multiplies this by 10, giving 9.2345. INT gives the whole number part of this which is 9, and so a 9 will be displayed. 9 is the highest number that can be displayed with this formula, because RAND does not actually give 1 as a random number. The highest number it will give is 0.9999..., 0.9999...×10= 9.999..., and the whole number part of this is 9.

Arithmetic practice

- Excel file

- available on accompanying CD, *Arithmetic_practice.xls*

- can be edited for use with all children who are learning to do addition, sub-traction, multiplication or division.

There are eight different worksheets in this file, which can be accessed by clicking on the tabs on the bottom of the window. Two give practice in addition, two in sub-traction, two in multiplication and two in division. *Add1* and *subtract1* involve numbers up to and including 20. *Add2* and *subtract2* use numbers up to and including 100. *Multiply1* and *divide1* use numbers up to and including 5. *Multiply2* and *divide2* use numbers up to and including 10. Figure 8.1 shows *add1* with the correct value filled in using the annotation tools. It also shows the onscreen key-board, which can be used to generate new questions by pressing F9. To find the function keys (normally at the top of a keyboard, above the numbers) on the ACTIVprimary onscreen keyboard, press the large F key on the top left of the adult keyboard first.

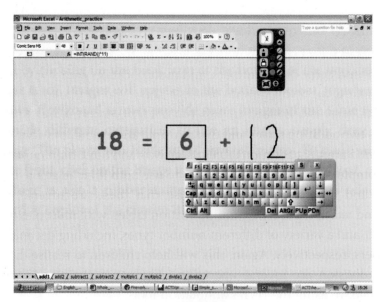

Figure 8.1 Addition practice

The purpose of this resource is to give quick practice to children in a variety of arithmetic sums at an appropriate level. They are deliberately written with the 'answer' on the left, and the calculation on the right. Numbers are selected at random by Excel, and new questions can be obtained by pressing F9 on the computer keyboard or on the onscreen keyboard. Children can either answer by all calling out the answer together, or by writing them down on individual whiteboards and holding them up. Having new questions available at the press of a key means that pace is maintained. All these worksheets can be edited to change the range of numbers used.

Changing the limits on the numbers

To change the limits on the numbers provided in a cell, select that cell, then go to the formula bar (at the top, with *fx* to its left). The formula in the cell will be displayed there, and can be edited either in the formula bar or in the cell itself.

The formula =INT(RAND()*11), which can be seen on the formula bar in Figure 8.1, produces a random whole number between 0 and 10. To change this to a random whole number between 0 and any other integer, just change the 11 to *one more* than the highest number required.

The formula =INT(RAND()*(21-10)+10) produces a random whole number between 20 and 10. To change the lowest number wanted, change both 10's to the required number; to change the highest number, change the 21 to *one more* than the highest number required.

Addition table

- Excel file

- resource available on accompanying CD, *Addition_table.xls*

- can be edited for all children who are learning to do addition and subtraction with two- and three-digit numbers, and multiplication with a variety of numbers.

This file has two addition tables and two multiplication tables of varying difficulty. *Add1* and *add2* are 5 × 5 addition tables using two- and three-digit numbers respectively. To complete them requires children to use both their addition and subtraction skills, and thus helps them to realise that these are inverse operations. *Multiply1* and *multiply2* are 5 × 5 multiplication tables, with multiples of numbers from 1 to 10, and a variety of different number types, including decimals and two-digit numbers, respectively. Again, this will help children to realise that multiplication and division are inverse operations. Figure 8.2 shows *add1* with some numbers filled in, using the IWB's annotation tools.

Figure 8.2 Addition table

To produce a new table, simply press the F9 key on the computer keyboard or the onscreen keyboard. This will cause all the numbers to change, so that you have a new resource available every time you want one. (Very occasionally, you may find that *add1* and *add2* give a larger or smaller number than indicated above, or even a negative number. If this happens, just press F9 again, to get a new table.) This resource can be done individually by children, or worked on as a collaborative task by the whole class. This gives the teacher the opportunity to discuss with the children which numbers can be found at any point, and how this might be done.

Checking answers does not require the teacher to work out all the questions, unless they want to! All the missing numbers are actually in the Excel spreadsheet, so the teacher can concentrate on helping children with difficulties. The answers cannot be seen because their font colour has been matched to that of the background. In Figure 8.3, the worksheet *multiply2* can be seen with the font colour changed to display the answers, and the annotated answers suggested by the class shown below.

Checking the answers

To see all the numbers in the table press Ctrl A on the keyboard, which selects the whole worksheet, then click on the A icon (underlined in black in Figure 8.3, on the right of the top toolbar). Choose a colour which will show up against the background colours, and all the fonts will change to this colour. To hide these numbers again, press Ctrl Z which will undo the font colour change.

On the SMARTboard

Annotated answers can be restored for comparison with the actual answers by pressing the Restore icon on the floating keyboard.

In ACTIVprimary

Restoring the annotated answers will not be possible until the new version of the software is available. If the children have written their answers on individual whiteboards, or on paper, they can compare their answers with those on the IWB. Alternatively, the completed table can be displayed on the IWB by using the Snapshot tool to copy the annotations onto the clipboard. These can then be pasted onto the spreadsheet, as in Figure 8.3. This shows the worksheet, *multiply2*, with the font colour changed to display the answers, and the annotated answers worked out by the class shown below. This was 'photographed' using the Snapshot tool, and the 'photo' pasted into the spreadsheet for comparison. When this has been done, the annotations can be deleted by clicking on them, and pressing the delete key on the keyboard.

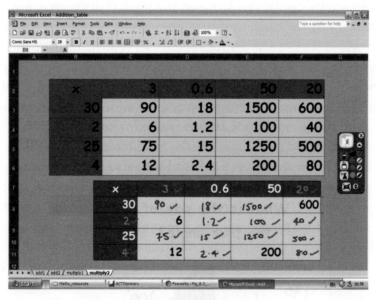

Figure 8.3 Checking answers in ACTIVprimary

Changing these resources is similar to the previous one. Certain of the numbers use random numbers provided by Excel, and you can change the lower and upper limits for these as described in the previous section. Just click on a cell to see if it contains a random number (shown by a formula beginning with =) or not. The other cells do not require change to edit the resource.

It is as well to test these tables thoroughly after any changes to make sure that the addition tables do not give the wrong type of numbers too frequently, or the multiplication tables provide calculations which are too difficult. Testing is best done on a trial and error basis by repeatedly pressing F9 and seeing what comes up. You may decide that an occasional table which is too difficult for some reason is not a problem, since another can be brought up very quickly instead.

Angle estimation

- Excel file
- resource available on accompanying CD, *Angle_estimation.xls*
- provides angles for estimation.

There are four versions of this resource in *Angle_estimation.xls*. The simplest version, *angle90,10* gives angles up to 90 degrees in multiples of 10 degrees. *Angle90,5* does the same thing but in multiples of 5 degrees, and *angle360,10* and *angle360,5* give angles up to 360 degrees in multiples of 10 and 5 degrees. F9 on the keyboard provides new angles, and the class can contribute answers to be put on the board, as in Figure 8.4, or they could write their estimates on individual whiteboards.

The correct angles can be displayed on the top left of the Window. The white rectangle containing the angle needs to be dragged out of the way, so that the answer is revealed (Figure 8.4). SMARTboard users can bring back annotations by using the Restore icon on the floating toolbox, whereas ACTIVprimary users will need to 'photo' the annotations to the clipboard using the Snapshot tool, and then paste them back into the spreadsheet to compare with the correct answer.

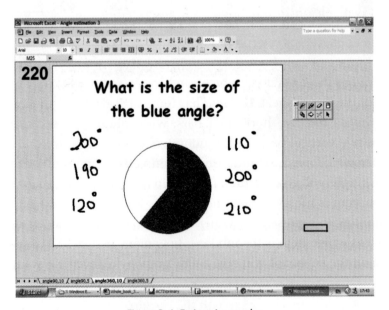

Figure 8.4 Estimating angles

How can Excel show angles?

This resource also relies on Excel's random number facility. At the top left, where the answer is displayed, a random number between 0 and 1 is generated, which is then scaled up so that it gives a whole number between 0 and 90 or 0 and 360 in the appropriate multiple.

For example, to produce whole numbers between 0 and 90 in 10 degree intervals, the formula used is =10*INT(RAND()*10). RAND()*10 gives a number somewhere between 0 and 10, but not including 10. INT then takes the whole number part of this, giving an integer between 0 and 9. This is then multiplied by 10 to give the required angle correct to the nearest ten. For angles between 0 and 360 degrees, at 5 degree intervals, the formula is =5*INT(RAND()*73).

The angle is then produced from a pie chart of the value given by this process, and 360 minus this value. The two are actually side by side at the top left of the Window, but the second value is obscured because it is in a font the same colour as the background. Selecting the two values, then clicking on the Chart icon on the toolbar at the top of the Window gives a box with a selection of different charts. Selecting Pie Charts gives a chart similar to the one displayed in this resource. Colour is changed by right-clicking on areas of the chart, which brings up a range of options. Format Data Point allows a section of the pie chart to be changed.

Interpreting graphs

- Excel file

- resource available on accompanying CD, *Interpreting_graphs.xls*

- provides bar charts for interpretation.

This resource has three versions, which can be accessed by clicking on the tabs at the bottom of the spreadsheet. *Graphs1* has four vertical bars, with random values up to 5. *Graphs2* has five horizontal bars, with random values up to 10, and *Graphs3* has five vertical bars, with random values up to 100 (in multiples of 5). Figure 8.5 shows *Graphs2*, with questions completed using the IWB annotation tools. These graphs will give children practice in interpreting bar charts. They need to see which item is most popular and which is least, and to find out how many people's opinion is represented. Other questions can be asked as the teacher wishes, such as which item is the mode, or how many people liked a specific item. Pressing F9 on the keyboard will give a new graph whenever it is wanted.

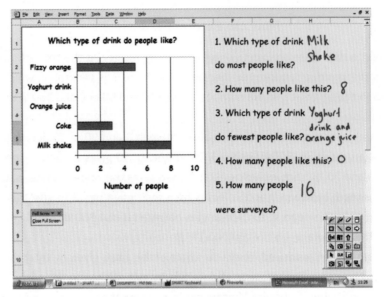

Figure 8.5 Interpreting bar graphs

To change the graphs

If you drag the graphs to the right, you will see two columns underneath. The left-hand column gives the items, such as fizzy orange, and so on; the right-hand column contains a formula which gives a random number. These can be changed to give different values as described in *Arithmetic Practice*.

To get a different type of graph, right click on the outer area of the graph, then select Chart Type from the pop-up menu. Different questions can be incorporated by typing them into the space on the right of the graph.

Presentations

How many?

- PowerPoint file

- resource available on accompanying CD, *How_many.ppt*

- can be edited for all children just learning to count.

This resource is for children in the early stages of learning to count. The numbers appear in order from 1 to 5. Children can count the images as they appear on the screen, and then see the figure and corresponding word.

To start this presentation, click or tap on the first slide. The number 1 will appear. Click on this and a new slide will appear. Click again, and a picture, a number 1 and the word 'one' will appear. When you are ready to move on, click on the number 1, to return to the first slide. Click again (not on the number 1), and a number 2 will appear. Continue in this way, clicking on the numbers to move from one slide to another.

Figure 8.6 Counting children

Changing this resource

Additional slides could be added, or images and text changed to provide variety. See *PowerPoint* in Chapter 5 for details on how to do this. The order of the slides can be changed by going to Slide Sorter View, and dragging the slides as required.

Counting

- PowerPoint file

- resource available on accompanying CD, *Counting.ppt*

- can be edited for use with all children just learning to count.

This presentation also uses clipart and Word art for the images and numbers. Tapping on the screen will bring up a question which the teacher can help the children to read. Another tap brings up the images, which everyone can count together. Finally the number appears. The file provided contains slides for the numbers 1 to 5, but not in numerical order.

Figure 8.7 Counting horses

Where's the triangle?

- PowerPoint file

- available on accompanying CD, *Wheres_the_triangle.ppt*

- can be edited for children beginning to learn about shapes.

This resource focuses children's attention on a specific shape, the triangle. The opening slide shows several triangles, so the lesson could start with a discussion of what a triangle looks like. On subsequent slides, triangles are incorporated into simple drawings for them to spot, as in Figure 8.8. In this particular slide, the triangle is 'upside down' – an opportunity to discuss whether triangles are still triangles this way up. Other slides have more than one triangle to spot.

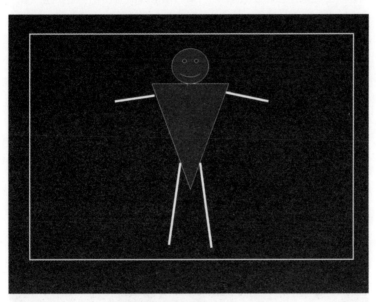

Figure 8.8 Where is the triangle?

Changing this resource

Additional slides could be added to provide variety. See *PowerPoint* in Chapter 5 for details on how to do this. Similar resources, but using other shapes, could be prepared in the same way. The drawings are put together using the Draw tools, which are available on the Draw toolbar at the bottom of the window in Slide View. If this is not visible, go to View>Toolbars, and select Drawing. The Draw toolbar contains shapes and lines, and allows different colours to be used for these, and to fill the shapes.

Time

- PowerPoint file

- resource available on accompanying CD, *Whats_the_ time.ppt*

- can be edited for children learning to tell the time.

In this file, several slides give children the opportunity to answer questions about the time. Some of the slides have a time displayed, while others show a time when the screen is tapped. All the slides have sound files attached, so that correct answers can be rewarded with clapping and cheering. Some sounds start automatically, others have a loudspeaker icon which should be clicked or tapped when a correct answer has been given.

Each slide has a question to answer, but other questions can be asked also, such as 'What will the time be in 1 hour?', 'What was the time half an hour ago?', and so on. Slides like these give good opportunities for differentiated questions to be asked. In the slide shown in Figure 8.9, the clock is initially without hands. As well as answering verbally what time they think it might be, children could come up to the board to draw hands on the clock corresponding to the time they think the pictures indicate. A click of the mouse then produces hands at half past twelve, and the loudspeaker icon can be clicked to produce applause (the time could be changed to dinner time in a particular school, by changing the orientation of the hands).

Figure 8.9 What's the time?

To change this resource

Different pictures can be added to the slides, to illustrate different times of day, and appropriate text added. The clock hand images currently shown can be changed to show different times, by rotating them.

Hands can be added if required by using the Draw toolbar. The straight line tool or the arrow tool can be used for the hands – the arrow tool has been used in this resource. The colour and thickness of the line or arrow can be changed as required, and the line or arrow moved by dragging, or rotated by dragging on one end of the line.

Special effects were added to the hands using Slide Show>Custom Animation from the top toolbar, and sound effects were added using Insert>Movies and Sounds>Sounds from Clip Organizer from the top toolbar. These were also animated using Custom Animation.

Ordering numbers

- IWB file

- available on accompanying CD, *Ordering_numbers.flp* or *Ordering_numbers.xbk*

- can be edited for children of all ages.

This resource contains numbers to order, some using number lines. It can be used with children of all ages by choosing appropriate numbers. The resource provided has numbers with one decimal place, but these can easily be edited to provide different numbers. Later pages contain numbers to be put in order without a number line.

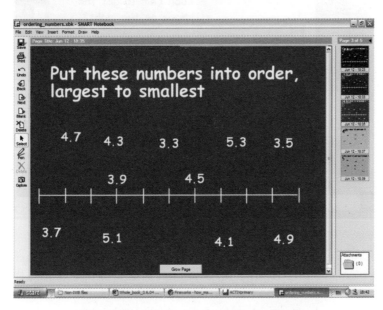

Figure 8.10 Ordering numbers on a number line

The number lines are prevented from moving, even if accidentally dragged by a child. The number lines are part of the background on the SMARTboard, and locked in place in the ACTIVprimary flipchart. This can be easily reversed in both cases if required.

Making the number lines

Number lines can be obtained in ACTIVprimary by clicking on the Library tool, then selecting Numeracy and Number Lines. A selection of number lines will appear in the bottom tool tray. In this resource, the blank number line has been used. This page could be saved as a page background if desired.

The number line on the SMARTboard was made by using a grid background, and drawing the number line using that as a guide. Only one vertical line was drawn, the rest were produced using copy and paste. The number line was then copied to a page with a plain coloured background. This could be saved as a page template if desired.

Shapes (reflection/rotation)

- IWB software

- resource available on accompanying CD, *Rotating_reflecting_shapes.flp* or *Rotating_reflecting_shapes.xbk*

- can be edited for children learning about rotating and reflecting shapes.

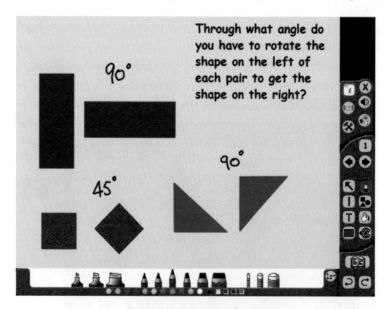

Figure 8.11 Rotating shapes

On the first page of this resource, three shapes are reproduced, and then rotated, as in Figure 8.11. The children have to decide what the angle of rotation is in each case. The left-hand shape can then be rotated to see if they were right.

Rotating shapes

In ACTIVprimary go into Design Mode, and click on the shape so that the resizing handles appear. There will also be a curved arrow on the right of the shape, which can be used to rotate the shape.

On a SMARTboard, tap on the shape so that the resizing handle appears. There will also be a green circle above the shape. This is a rotation handle.

In ACTIVprimary, judging the angle of rotation is made easy, because when any shape is rotated, a meter appears in the top left-hand corner of the screen, which records the angle of rotation. On a SMARTboard, the angle of rotation will have to be measured in some other way, such as in half and quarter turns. If the left-hand shape needs a quarter turn to look like the right-hand shape, then the angle of rotation is 90 degrees.

On the second page of this resource, pairs of shapes are shown with a straight line between them. Children have to drag one shape into the right place so that each is a reflection of the other in the straight line. Squared grid backgrounds are provided to help with this activity. Neither ACTIVprimary nor SMARTboard software provides a mechanism for flipping the shapes over to check if the shapes have been correctly placed, so this will have to be judged by the teacher.

Producing the shapes

In ACTIVprimary, click on the shapes icon on the vertical toolbar. This will give a selection of shapes in the bottom toolbar. If the required shape does not appear, use the vertical navigation arrow on the right-hand side of this toolbar, and select the type of shape required. Colours can also be chosen.

On the SMARTboard, the square and rectangle were produced using the Draw>Rectangle menu. The triangle was produced using the Draw>Shapes menu. In each case, the Format menu was used for the line colour and the Fill colour.

Fraction wall

- IWB software

- resource available on accompanying CD, *Fraction_wall.xbk* or *Fraction_wall.flp*

- can be edited for children learning about fractions.

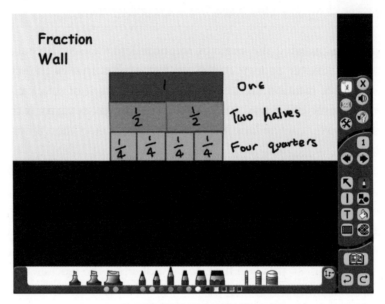

Figure 8.12 Fraction wall

IWB software can be used for all kinds of work on fractions. This fraction wall (Figure 8.12) was made by using the rectangle tool to make different sized rectangles, which were then duplicated as needed. Similar fraction walls can be made for any other set of fractions. ACTIVprimary contains a fraction tool in the Special Tools which gives realistic fraction notation, although this can only be used with a board, and cannot be used with a computer alone in preparation. In Figure 8.12, the Reveal/Screen Shade tool has been used to hide part of the screen. The shade can be pulled down bit by bit to reveal the next row of fractions.

These fraction walls have the additional advantage of not being static. The rectangles can be moved onto each other to show the relationships between them, such as a quarter is half of a half. They can also be resized to show that the relationships still hold true when the whole is changed to something else. To do this, group the objects so that they all change in the same way.

Once children have become familiar with the basic relationships between fractions, fraction walls can be used to help them understand the arithmetic of fractions, such as $\frac{1}{2} + \frac{1}{4} = \frac{3}{4}$.

Making a simple fraction wall

This can be quickly made out of rectangles, using a grid background. In the resources given on the CD, the grid background has been removed. To replace it in ACTIVprimary, click on the Grid icon, and then select the grid and grid colour required. On a SMARTboard, use Ctrl A to select everything on a page, then Ctrl X to remove the page contents onto the clipboard. Insert>Browse for page template will give you the choice of various grids. A grid will appear on a new page, and the contents of the previous page can then be pasted (Ctrl V) onto the new page.

Fractions

- IWB software

- resource available on accompanying CD, *Fractions.flp* or *Fractions.xbk*

- can be edited for all children beginning fraction arithmetic.

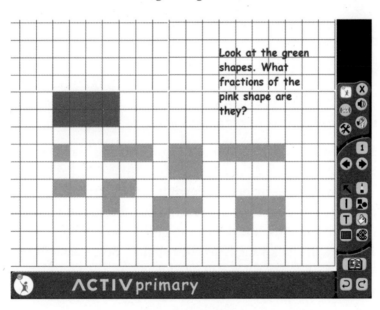

Figure 8.13 Fractions

In this resource, the green shapes are fractions of the pink shapes. Children can start by finding out what these fractions are. This can be done by dragging the green shapes onto the pink shape. All the shapes are slightly transparent so that the outline of the grid can be seen through them. The shapes can then be used to explore equivalent fractions, or addition and subtraction of fractions. The shapes in Figure 8.13, for instance, show that $^2/_8$ is the same as $^1/_4$, that $^4/_8$ is the same as $^1/_2$, and so on. This resource can also be used to help children with common misconceptions, such as adding the numerators and the denominators when they add two fractions. Two quarters ($^1/_4 + ^1/_4$) is clearly equal to $^4/_8$ rather than $^2/_8$. Resources like this help children to contextualise fractions and their arithmetic, rather than treating them as abstract problems, where questions and answers have no meaning.

Creating the shapes

In ACTIVprimary, start by clicking on the backgrounds icon, and choosing a squared grid. Then click on the shapes icon, and drag squares of a suitable colour onto the flipchart. These can be resized as required. To make them transparent, go into Design Mode, double click on the shape, and then click on the right-hand icon on the pop-up toolbar, Object Properties. This gives a dialogue box in which one of the options is Translucency. In the resource on the CD, this is set at about 66, but can be set as required.

On a SMARTboard, the rectangular shapes are created by using Draw>Rectangle, and choosing suitable colours, then resizing the rectangle as required. The SMARTboard software does not allow non-rectangular shapes like those in Figure 8.13 to be created as a single object. These were made from rectangles put together, then grouped using Ctrl G. Transparency is obtained by using Format>Transparency, and choosing the degree of transparency required. 25% is used in the resource on the CD, but this can be changed.

Pictograms

- IWB software

- resources available on accompanying CD, *Cars_pictogram.xbk* and *Cars_pictogram.flp*, *Pets_pictogram.xbk* and *Pets_pictogram.flp*

- can be edited to use with children of all ages creating pictograms.

Graphs of all kinds benefit by being shown in IWB software. It is difficult when drawing graphs freehand on an ordinary whiteboard to get all the lines where they should be. With pictograms, it is difficult to get all the symbols looking the same. On an IWB all graphs look exactly as they should. Some schools may have specialist software which helps teachers and children to produce pictograms immediately, but if your school does not have such software, these resources help you to create your own.

With younger children, you might want to put together a pictogram from information discussed verbally. In *Cars_pictogram*, different coloured car icons are chosen to represent the cars in the car park outside the school. Children can count the number of cars of each colour and icons can be added to the graph as they count. Figure 8.14 shows an example.

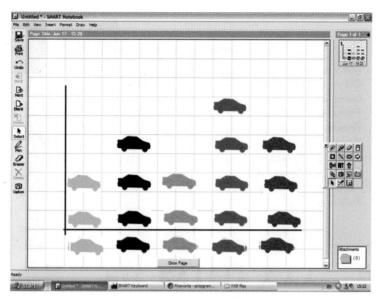

Figure 8.14 Pictogram showing the colours of cars in the car park

Creating the icons

In ACTIVprimary, a suitable picture of a car was chosen from the resource library. Using the pen tool, a point-to-point outline was drawn around this. The outline was then filled in with the Fill tool. Finally, a duplicate was made of the car, and a different colour used with the Fill tool. This can be repeated to make cars of any colour. The cars were then placed along the bottom axis of the graph. They were then duplicated and dragged into position to make the pictogram. To save these icons for another occasion, open up the Library, select which folder you want them to go into, and drag them into the library resources in the bottom toolbar.

On a SMARTboard, a suitable picture of a car was chosen from the clip-art library. Using the straight line tool, an outline was drawn around it. Although the Fill tool cannot be used to colour in the car, if a fairly thick line is chosen this is more than adequate to make an icon for a particular colour of car. Once one was made, it was copied, and the colour changed as required. The cars were then placed along the bottom axis of the graph, where they could be duplicated and dragged into position to make the pictogram. To save these icons for another occasion, save them into a clip-art folder.

For older children, making a pictogram could be part of a longer exercise in collecting data and presenting it. Prepare in advance a page with all the children's names ready, as in Figure 8.15. Ask each child how many pets their family owns, and fill in the appropriate number by their name. This information can then be transferred to a tally, and finally to a frequency table, as in Figure 8.15.

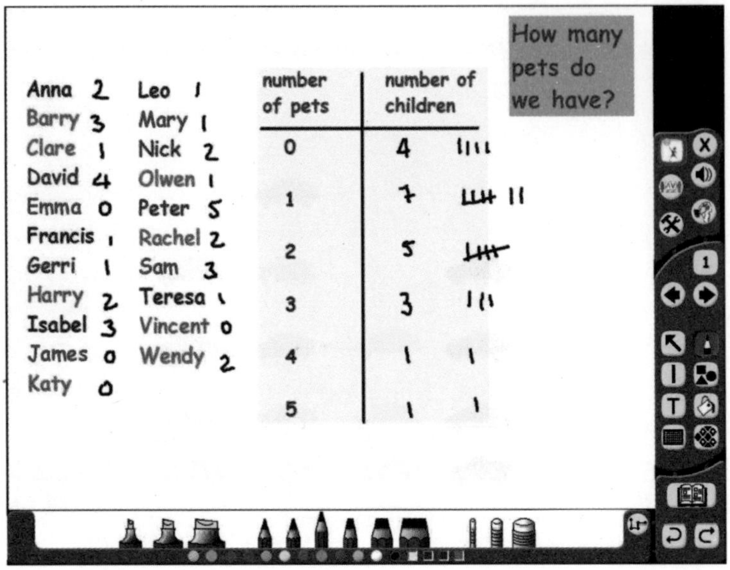

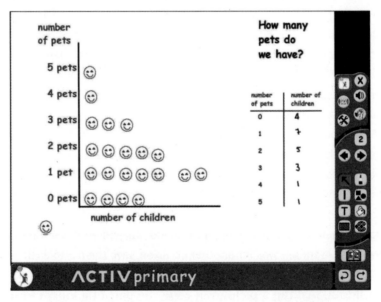

Figure 8.15 Collecting data for a tally and frequency table

The frequency table can then be copied onto the next page, where axes and icons are set out, ready for the graph to be constructed. In ACTIVprimary, the frequency table was copied using the Snapshot tool (obtained by clicking on the Special Tools icon). SMARTboards can use copy and paste or the Screen Capture tool.

Figure 8.16 Pictogram showing how many pets each child has

Creating the icon

In both ACTIVprimary and on the SMARTboard the face icon was created by using a pink circle, blue filled circles (slightly elongated) and a mouth drawn in red using the pen tool. Once created, it was copied using the Screen Capture/Snapshot tool, so that it was a single object, which could then be duplicated as required.

Geoboard activity

- IWB software

- resource available on accompanying CD, *Geoboards.xbk* or *Geoboards.flp*

- can be edited for use with children of all ages learning about shapes.

Simple 2×2 or 3×3 geoboards can be made up to use for whole class discussion, then printed out for follow-up work using real geoboards. Figure 8.17 shows sets of 3×3 geoboards which could be used to generate discussion about triangles. 'What is a triangle?', 'Are these all triangles?', 'Are any of them the same?', 'Could you change one into another by rotating it?', 'How many different triangles can you draw on a 3×3 geoboard?' and so on.

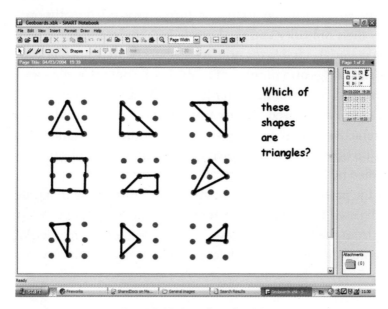

Figure 8.17 A geoboard activity

Creating the geoboards

On the SMARTboard, a grid background was used which helped to put the dots in the right places. One dot was made using a thick pen width, and the circle tool. This was then copied twice to make a row, and that was copied twice to make one geoboard (nine dots in a square). This was then converted to a group and copied twice more, to make a row of geoboards. Rows were then copied as required. Finally, all the geoboards were copied onto a new, blank page, and saved as a page template for future use (File>Save Page as Template).

In ACTIVprimary, a grid background was used, and a red circle chosen from the Resources Library, and resized. It was then duplicated twice to give a row of dots, which was then duplicated twice to make a single geoboard (nine dots in a square). This was copied twice more to make a row of geoboards. Rows were then copied as required. Finally, the background was changed to a plain background, and the page saved into the Background Library for future use ('photographed' with the Snapshot tool, then dragged into the Background Library).

Converting a webpage into an IWB resource

The Nrich website provides a huge resource bank of problems suitable for primary age children, which can be found at http://www.nrich.maths.org. These are arranged by their difficulty and the knowledge required to solve them. The First Tier has the material suitable for primary school children, and clicking on the link to the First Tier brings up a number of problems at content levels 1 and 2, and with difficulties which range from one star to three stars.

Some of these can be used directly from the IWB with the whole class, particularly the interactive games. A link towards the bottom right-hand side of the home page brings up *Games from the archive*, and a huge number of games can be found there, classified by their content and difficulty.

Some of the problems, however, might require displaying in a different way if they are to be used for whole class activity, as text is sometimes too small for children to see from the back of the class. This can be done using the IWB software, in the same way that an old worksheet or transparency can be revamped.

Decorating biscuits

- website used in preparation, plus IWB software

- example available on accompanying CD, *Biscuits.flp* or *Biscuits.xbk*

- editing a website for whole class use could be used with any webpage not suitable as it stands

- this particular problem is suitable for children looking at patterns in multiplication tables.

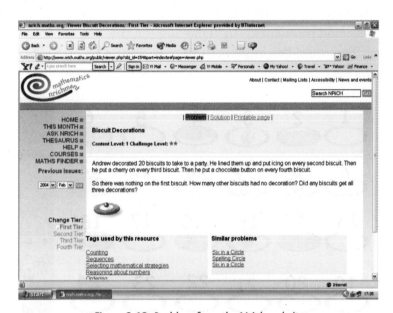

Figure 8.18 Problem from the Nrich website

It is not very easy to read the webpage shown in Figure 8.18, and it would be very difficult to read it from the back of the classroom. There is also information on the page which is not relevant. However, this problem can easily be adapted using IWB software for use with a whole class.

The problem is as follows:

Andrew decorated 20 biscuits to take to a party. He lined them up and put icing on every second biscuit. Then he put a cherry on every third biscuit. Then he put a chocolate button on every fourth biscuit.

So there was nothing on the first biscuit. How many other biscuits had no decoration? Did any biscuits get all three decorations?

The resource is created over two pages. On the first are ten biscuits, with cherries, icing and chocolate drops for the children to drag onto the biscuits. The stage is set for children to come up to the IWB, and drag the icing, cherries and chocolate drops onto the biscuits. This can then lead to discussion about which biscuits will not get any decoration, and which will get all three. In the first ten, no biscuits get all three – will that change with the second set of ten?

The second page has 24 biscuits laid out in lines of 6 (rather than 20 in lines of 5 or 10) so that children can see the patterns (see Figure 8.19). Looking at patterns in multiplication tables in this way will help children to understand this problem better, and the relationships between numbers. They can discuss which biscuits will not get any decoration, and which will get all three. Why do the 1st, 5th, 7th, 11th, and so on, get no decorations at all? Is it because they are prime numbers? (No, because 1 is not prime, and 2 and 3 did get decorations.) What is special about the 12th, the 24th, and so on? The problem could be extended by using a number square laid out in rows of 6 or 12, as in Figure 8.20 (this number square can be downloaded from the DfES Standards website, see Appendix 1 for details).

These pages could be adapted (by removing the cherries, chocolate drops and icing) so that they could be printed out as a worksheet for individual follow-up work.

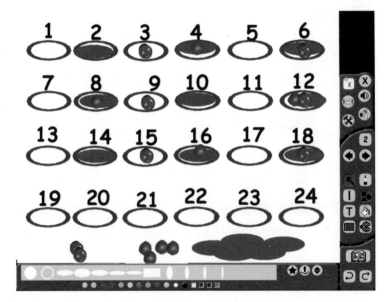

Figure 8.19 Decorating biscuits

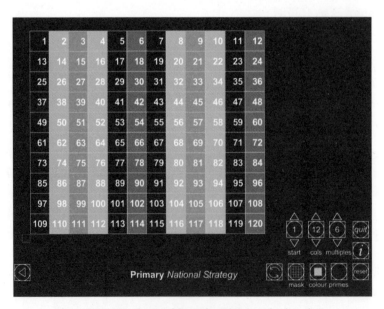

Figure 8.20 Number grid from the DfES Standards website

Creating the resource
ACTIVprimary

The biscuit is a useful illustration, so the first thing to do is to photo it using the Snapshot tool from the Special Tools. However, this already has icing and a cherry on it, so I used brown ellipses taken from the Shapes Library for a basic biscuit, which could then be decorated by the children. One biscuit could be duplicated to make two, and these duplicated to make four, and so on.

The icing was made by using a filled pink ellipse from the Shapes Library. The cherry and chocolate drop were made by photographing a cherry and a hazel nut (it looked just like a chocolate drop when edited!) found in the Resource Library.

SMARTboard

The biscuit is a useful illustration, so the first thing to do is to photo it using the Screen Capture tool. However, this already has icing and a cherry on it, so I used brown ellipses taken from the Draw menu for a basic biscuit, which could then be decorated by the children. One biscuit could be duplicated to make two, and these duplicated to make four, and so on.

The icing was made by using a filled pink ellipse from the Draw menu. The cherry and chocolate drop were made by photographing suitable pictures from the clip-art folders.

CHAPTER 9

Other subject areas

As with the resources in Chapters 7 and 8, these resources demonstrate techniques that could be used in a variety of different curriculum areas, and for children of all ages. They range from very simple resources, which would take virtually no time to make, to a long presentation which would take a substantial amount of time to prepare. If this is done with a class, however, it could form part of their ICT and other subject work, rather than being a drain on the teacher's time.

Quick resources

Where do our letters come from?

- IWB software

- example available on accompanying CD, *Letters.xbk* or *Letters.flp*

- can be edited for use for children learning about maps.

Most IWB software includes maps of the UK and usually of Europe and the world as well. These can be used to facilitate many activities which involve a map. *Letters* is an example of one such activity.

Children should bring into school envelopes which have clear postmarks. Working in small groups with a map of the UK, they can then find out where their envelopes came from, and where these places are on the map. Maps for them to record these places on can be printed out from the IWB. Once a group has worked out where all their envelopes are from, and marked them on their own maps, they can copy the information on the map on the IWB. Eventually a map of many different places in the UK will be built up, which can be discussed with the whole class. Each child could perhaps say where the envelope came from and who sent it, so that the map acquires personal significance for the class.

Labelling geographical features

- IWB software

- examples available on accompanying CD, *Geog_scenes1.xbk* or *Geog_scenes1.flp*, and *Geog_scenes2.xbk* or *Geog_scenes2.flp*

- can be edited to use for any situation where scenes or features require labelling in Geography, Science or other curriculum areas.

A picture or diagram of geographical features can be labelled, with children either dragging ready-prepared labels to the corresponding pictures, or erasing layers hiding labels, so that the labels are revealed. The examples on the CD contain digital photos. These could be changed for other photos, or for diagrams, as required.

Figure 9.1 shows four different geographical settings, with labels to drag onto the correct scene. Figure 9.2 shows very similar settings, but this time the labels are typed in, then almost covered over, using an annotation pen in the same colour as the background. After discussion about what the labels might be, the covering layer can be removed with the eraser tool. These resources could be a stimulus for discussion about the different settings, what features we might expect them to show, what features they would not show, and so on.

Figure 9.1 Matching labels and pictures

Figure 9.2 Revealing labels

Presentations requiring more preparation

Food from abroad

- Science/Geography/Citizenship curriculum areas
- uses IWB software and scanned images or digital photos
- resource available on accompanying CD, *our_food.flp* or *our_food.xbk*

Where does our food come from? This question could be explored as part of the geography curriculum, with references to social and scientific issues. The resource on the CD uses a poster which was available from Oxfam (now out of print). The first page of the resource uses the whole poster to support a general discussion with the children about where they think their food comes from, how it gets to them, and so on.

Each scene in the poster (Figure 9.3) is linked to a page which shows that picture on its own with questions to consider. What part of the world does this food come from? How is it grown? What is the climate like there? What are the conditions for the people there? In the ACTIVprimary flipchart, the pictures of the food production scenes on the first page are linked to the appropriate pages, and the same scenes on their individual pages are linked back to the main page. Clicking on the photos opens the next page in the sequence. In the SMARTboard notebook, navigation needs to be done using the small page icons on the right-hand side of the screen.

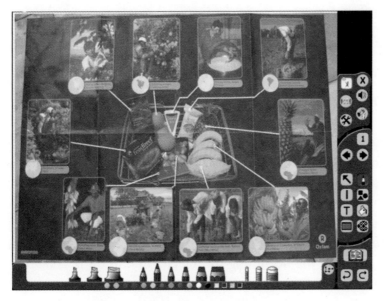

Figure 9.3 Where does our food come from?

Using a poster

The poster could either be scanned into the computer in sections or photographed with a digital camera. Scanned images will need to be reduced in size, either using Paint or similar software, or by resizing in the IWB software. Alternatively, sections of a poster could be scanned or photographed to make them into digital images.

Creating links to other pages

In ACTIVprimary, each of the individual pictures was photographed separately using a digital camera, and that image imposed on that of the whole poster. The reason for this was so that the software would recognise each picture as a separate object. Next, each picture was double-clicked so that the floating toolbar appeared, and Object properties was selected. There is an option here to link an object to a different page in a flipchart.

On the SMARTboard, this cannot be done, so the page views on the right-hand side of the screen are used for navigation.

The Solar System

- Science curriculum

- PowerPoint file, plus photographs downloaded from the internet

- resource available on accompanying CD, *The_Solar_System.ppt.*

Astronomy is frequently in the news these days, and is a great way to motivate children to find out more about science. The NASA website contains a wealth of photos of astronomical features and events which are freely available for schools to use (see Appendix 1 for details). A PowerPoint or IWB resource can be put together using these as illustrations.

The resource on the CD describes the solar system, using photos from the web. Questions are set at the beginning for the children to think about as they watch the presentation, and these are then repeated at the end for them to answer. Questions range from facts and figures (which is the hottest, the largest, and so on) to whether Pluto and Sedna are planets at all. This could be followed by research on the internet into interesting aspects of the solar system.

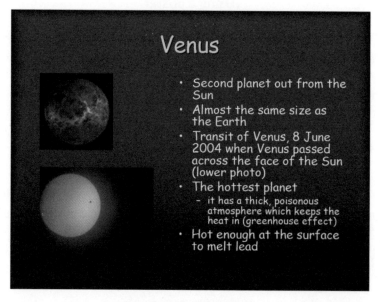

Figure 9.4 The Solar System

Resources like this can be put together quickly in PowerPoint using the internet as a source of illustrations. Pictures are readily available on the web (although note copyright restrictions in Appendix 1), allowing any teacher to put together a resource which is directly relevant to the needs of their class, but is attractive and professional looking.

Plants

- Science curriculum

- IWB software plus digital photographs

- resource available on accompanying CD, *Plants.flp* or *Plants.xbk.*

Presentation software using digital photos can be used to help young children identify and label parts of plants, and to answer questions about them. These files were created by photographing plants of various types with a digital camera, then cropping and resizing the images to fit the IWB pages. The first image (Figure 9.5) is the usual stylised picture of a flowering plant often seen in books.

Figure 9.5   A flowering plant

This image has labels which can be dragged to the right part of the image by the children, and includes alternative names for the stem of the flower. The following pages contain pictures of flowers, leaves, buds and seeds which are a little more unusual than this to stimulate discussion about the different types of parts of a plant found, and perhaps to discuss their function in general terms. Photos can include garden plants, hedgerow plants, weeds, houseplants and trees, so that children can see that these all come under the general heading of plants.

Two pages are illustrated in Figure 9.6 and Figure 9.7, one containing labels to be dragged to appropriate parts of the image, and one with a question to discuss. These are straightforward to produce, requiring only digital photos with brief labels added. Children could bring in plants of their own to talk about as well. This resource can easily be changed to suit the requirements of any particular class, by simply changing the photos and text.

Figure 9.6 A flowering cactus

Figure 9.7 An unusual plant

Food groups

- Science/PSHE curriculum

- uses IWB software and digital photographs

- resource available on accompanying CD, *Food_groups.xbk* or *Food_groups.flp*.

What does our food contain? What things are good for us, which less so? This topic can be explored using IWB software. The resource is straightforward to set up. A hexagon, with sections for each of the major food categories, was drawn onto the first page (taken from the Resource Library in ACTIVprimary, or Draw>Shapes on the SMARTboard) and then copied onto a second page. This could be extended to as many pages as are required. Pictures of different food items were taken with a digital camera, and cropped and reduced in size (this can be done in Paint, if your digital camera software does not contain a picture editing package), so that several pictures could be put round the hexagon, as in Figure 9.8.

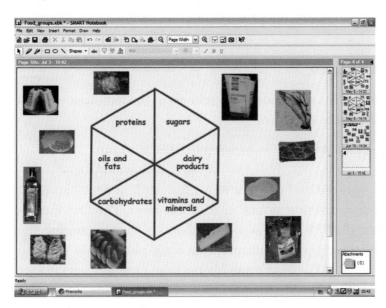

Figure 9.8 Food groups

Children could take it in turns to move pictures into the appropriate section of the hexagon. This allows discussion of what each food contains, what type of food it is, whether it contains more than one food type, whether it should be part of a healthy diet, and so on. If the class decides that, for instance, nuts should be in two sections of the hexagon, since they contain both proteins and oils, then a copy can be made quickly, using the IWB software, so that they can be put in both categories. The activity could be extended by choosing the components of several meals from the pictures, and then comparing which gave a balanced variety of foods and which did not.

Children could take part in making a similar resource of their own by bringing in foods from home, and taking the pictures, then cropping them and reducing them in size for themselves, giving experience with using a digital camera, and preparing photos for use in a different ICT medium as well.

Creating a major presentation

The Ely Story

- Geography/History/English/ICT/Citizenship curriculum areas

- IWB software plus digital photographs

- this will take several lessons to create if used as an ICT lesson or as part of a geographical study

- could be used for a local study for schools in the fens area, or as a contrasting study for schools elsewhere

- example available on accompanying CD, *Ely_story.ppt*.

The file *Ely_story.ppt* has been created to illustrate how a major presentation might be put together, covering several curriculum areas. The first five slides run one after another. The fifth slide has a set of photos of the area around Ely (taken from the top of the towers of the Cathedral – an aerial photo could also be used to show an area in this way). Some of these photos have numbers next to them, and these photos should be tapped in turn to link forward to a slide about that area. All the photos on the slides after this have hyperlinks which link back to the main page, so that the link from the next photo can be chosen.

Inserting hyperlinks in PowerPoint

Select the photo or piece of text to which the hyperlink is to be attached. Go to Insert>Hyperlink or press Ctrl K on the keyboard. A box will appear, and another slide can be chosen, or another file elsewhere on the computer. To operate the hyperlink, simply tap on the object. A hand will appear indicating that there is a live hyperlink.

In the Geography and History curriculum areas, children are required to do a local study and to study local issues. Such topics could enable a class to create a major presentation, which could then be displayed at an Assembly or at a Parents' Evening. Researching and putting together the presentation would involve the children in a variety of local issues and in developing their use of ICT. Doing a presentation to the rest of the school and/or to parents involves putting together a script and public speaking, which are part of the English curriculum. Depending on your local area, other areas of the curriculum could also be involved, particularly citizenship issues.

A major presentation like this needs careful planning, which could be part of the learning experience for the children. A possible breakdown of the stages could be:

Stage 1: creation of a story board with the children

- use of websites and books to find out about the local area

- main stages in the history of the area

- how the history affects the geography

- main geographical features to be included

- what to find where in the area

- creating the story that the presentation will tell.

Stage 2: planning the presentation with the children

- is it going to be created in PowerPoint or with IWB software?

- what slides/pages are needed?

- detailed composition of each slide/page

- who is going to do what?

Stage 3: collecting resources

- what photos do we need?

- are other physical resources needed as well as photos?

- who is going to get what?

Stage 4: putting it all together

- groups of children each create a slide/page

- pictures, text, special effects included.

Stage 5: display at an Assembly or Parents' Evening

- who is going to do the presentation?

- a speaker from each group perhaps?

- putting together a script

- rehearsing

- doing it!

To illustrate how such a resource might be put together, I have created a presentation on the City of Ely and its surrounding area, showing each of these stages and how the IWB might be used to facilitate the project. The resource on the CD, *Ely_story.ppt*, is the result.

Stage 1: creation of a story board for the presentation

The geography of the City of Ely and the surrounding fens is man-made, so the geography and history of the area are interdependent. Originally, the City of Ely was known as the Isle of Ely, because it rose out of the surrounding marshes. The people lived with the water, eating fish and eels (hence the name of 'Ely'), using reeds to make houses and boats, walking on stilts in the marshes, travelling by boat.

After the Norman invasion in the 11th century, there was a strong resistance movement in the area, led by the Saxon leader, Hereward the Wake. Hereward and his followers exploited the local geography, and the general remoteness of the area, preventing William the Conqueror and his army from moving along the causeways, sabotaging wooden rafts, and setting bridges alight.

However, some monks at Ely monastery gave information to William, and eventually he was able to subdue the area. The monastery at Ely was extremely rich at the time, and William made them pay £1000 (a lot of money in those days) as a penalty for the City's resistance. The Cathedral was started by William on the site of the former Saxon monastery once the area was subdued, as a symbol of his authority.

The story of Ely then jumps to the time of Oliver Cromwell in the 17th century. Oliver came from nearby Huntingdon, but lived in Ely for many years, where he was the local MP. Oliver was part of the Parliament which opposed Charles I, leading to the Civil War and Charles' execution. Although not originally a soldier, Oliver fought bravely for the Parliamentary side (the 'Roundheads'), eventually becoming a prominent leader. He was one of the 59 people to sign the king's death warrant. A few years after the death of Charles I, Cromwell became the Lord Protector of England during the few years when England was a republic.

Up until this time, the fens around Ely had been very inhospitable, and useless for farming. The Romans had tried to build a drainage system, but it was not very extensive and fell into disuse after they left. Serious attempts to drain the fens were not made again until the Civil War in the 17th century. A Dutch engineer, Vermuyden, was brought in to do the job, together with immigrant Dutch labour. They cut new channels, draining the excess water from the land.

As a result, much rich peat soil was uncovered, which proved to be extremely fertile. However, drying out the soil made it sink, and many of the rivers and channels are now considerably above the level of the surrounding land. The characteristic appearance of the fens around Ely is entirely man-made.

In the City of Ely itself, early development was in the area around the Cathedral, where important landmarks are the Cathedral itself, and Cromwell's house. Just beyond the Cathedral, Market Square has been the site of a busy market since mediaeval times. The River Ouse was an important means of transport, so development occurred along the river and between the Cathedral and the river. Once roads were established, further development occurred along these roads. Since the late 20th century, Ely has expanded rapidly with the development of science and technology parks north of Cambridge, and there are many new housing developments being built right up to the present day.

Stage 2: Creating a presentation

The basic story has just been outlined. This story in itself shows many opportunities to explore the local history and geography, and how they affect each other. The nature of the mediaeval fens allowed Hereward the Wake to lead resistance against William the Conqueror, draining the fens created the characteristic geography we now see. Each area will have its own story like this to uncover and explore with the children.

The next stage is to plan a presentation. What kind of software will be used? Which episodes will be used to give detail and explain the story? A design for each slide/page will need to be planned. How much text will there be, how many pictures? Who will do what?

What software will be used? PowerPoint is a good medium for this kind of presentation, as is IWB software. Here, this resource has been prepared with PowerPoint, as it is easier to create hyperlinks between pictures and other pages in the resource in PowerPoint.

The major incidents in the story above are the Saxon resistance to William the Conqueror under Hereward the Wake, the building of the Cathedral, Oliver Cromwell, the draining of the fens, and the subsequent development of the City. These have been used to create PowerPoint slides. Photos and pictures of local places are used to illustrate the story, with brief comments. A more detailed story (as presented above) could then be written for children to present when they display their presentation.

Stage 3: Collecting resources

Once the class has decided who is going to create each slide and what its content will be, the children need to work out what pictures and photos they need, whether they want other artefacts, and how these are going to be collected. There will inevitably be constraints on what is practical. Is a digital camera available? Can the children borrow it over a weekend to take photos for their page, or do some have access to digital cameras at home? Do some children have old photos that could be scanned into the computer? Is a field trip to look at certain areas and take photos possible? Once the basic story has been discussed, a field trip would certainly help to bring it alive.

Stage 4: Putting it all together

Each group of children will need time together at the computer or IWB to design their page. An initial design can be done on paper, once they know what pictures they have available.

Stage 5: Doing the presentation

A detailed script should be put together, with each child knowing what he or she is going to say, how to operate the IWB, and having rehearsed their part. Links from one slide to another can be activated by tapping on the appropriate part of the slide either with a finger or with the pen, as in *Ely.ppt*.

A major activity like this allows several curriculum areas to be linked together, with the IWB used to help children create a resource which they will be proud to demonstrate at an Assembly or to their parents. Afterwards, it can be printed out and made into a class book, so that a permanent record is kept of the children's work.

Where to get help and find additional resources

DfES

The Standards Site of the DfES has many Numeracy resources which can be used on an IWB. These can be downloaded from http://www.standards.dfes.gov.uk/numeracy/publications/

Becta

Becta (British Educational Communications and Technology Agency), the ICT wing of the DfES, has many resources. These range from booklets on how to get the most out of your IWB, to what research says about IWB use, to subject specific booklets.

Find out what they have at: http://www.ictadvice.org.uk/

National Whiteboard Network

Information about IWBs and software available at http://nwnet.org.uk/pages/index.html. They also have resources to download for Maths and English, together with information on how to incorporate ICT across the curriculum.

IWB manufacturers' websites

Promethean's website has an area for users of their software. Go to http://www.promethean.co.uk/index.htm, click on Main Menu>ACTIVsoftware users group. This contains ideas from teachers, help with technical and pedagogical issues, and much more.

Details of how to use SMARTboard software, plus downloads of the latest version of the software can be obtained from http://www.smarttech.com/sbsoftware/index.asp

Other websites

NASA has a huge range of photographs of the planets, and everything else to do with space science. These are all in the public domain, which means that schools can use them freely. This particular site is good for planets:
http://pds.jpl.nasa.gov/planets/

The Nrich website at http://www.nrich.maths.org has a wide range of mathematical problems, games and activities, some of which would be very suitable for use on an IWB.

The following websites have resources for use on IWBs. They are not necessarily the best to be found, but they will help get you started.
http://smarteducation.org.uk
http://www.espresso.co.uk/services/primary/
http://www.ict.oxon-lea.gov.uk/whiteboards.html
http://www.primaryresources.co.uk/online/
http://www.mape.org.uk/activities/index.htm
http://www.interactive-resources.co.uk/
http://www.bgfl.org/bgfl/custom/resources_ftp/client_ftp/teacher/other/wboard_env/
http://www.edcompass.co.uk/

Copyright

Most pictures on the internet will not be in the public domain, and there will be copyright restrictions on their use. Before using a photo, check to see who owns the copyright and what restrictions there are. If you want to use a photo, you can always email the copyright owner and ask for permission.

Reference Table for ACTIVprimary version 1.1.23, 2004

Note   Text in **bold** type: Function
          Text in parentheses: Where to find the function

Backgrounds   (Vertical toolbar) Range of backgrounds appears in bottom toolbar. Use navigation arrows for more of current type, or different types.

Calculator   (Vertical toolbar, special tools) 2nd from right. Two versions. Both are 'simple' calculators, so correct order of operations needs to be entered.

Clear screen   (Annotation tools) Clears all annotations and returns you to open document.

Copy object to the clipboard   (Design mode) Right click, select Copy.

Delete an object   Click an object, select dustbin.

Design mode   (Vertical toolbar, Promethean man, Teacher tools) 2nd icon from right should be red.

Desktop capture   (Vertical toolbar, Promethean man, Teachers toolbar) 3rd icon from right. Returns to other applications.

Dice   (Vertical toolbar, special tools) 3rd icon from left.

Duplicate object   Click on object. Select two-column icon.

Fill   (Vertical toolbar) Colours appear in bottom toolbar. Use to fill shapes or as background colour. Click on area to be filled.

Fraction tool   (Vertical toolbar, special tools) 4th icon from right. Can only be used with board attached.

Grids   (Vertical toolbar) Provides a range of grids and lines.

Handwriting recognition   (Special tools, vertical toolbar) 'ab' icon in bottom toolbar. Requires attached board to function.

New flipchart   (Teachers toolbar, Promethean man, vertical toolbar) 1st icon on left.

Next page   (Vertical toolbar) Right pointing arrow.

Open flipchart   (Teachers toolbar, Promethean man, vertical toolbar) 2nd icon on left.

Page notes   (Vertical toolbar, Promethean man, Teacher tools) 4th icon from right.

Page organiser   (Design mode, vertical toolbar page selector) Page organiser icon at right of bottom toolbar. Clicking on this opens up page organiser.

Page selector   (Vertical toolbar) Number of current page. Clicking on this opens up page selector in bottom toolbar.

Paste object from the clipboard   (Design mode) Right click, select Paste object.

Pens, highlighters and erasers   (Annotation tools) Appear when AP is open, and another application is accessed. Can be used to annotate any application, including web pages.

Pens, highlighters and erasers   (Vertical toolbar) Range of pen, highlighter, eraser widths and colours will appear in bottom toolbar. Use Draw point to point for straight lines.

Presentation mode   (Vertical toolbar, Promethean man, Teacher tools) 2nd icon from right should be yellow.

Previous page   (Vertical toolbar) Left pointing arrow.

Print flipchart   (Vertical toolbar, Promethean man, Teachers toolbar) 4th icon from left.

Protractor   (Vertical toolbar, special tools) 4th icon from left.

Reset the page   (Vertical toolbar, Promethean man, Teacher tools) 5th icon from left.

Resizing an object   (Presentation mode) Click on object, select + or −.

Resizing an object   (Design mode) Click on object, select + or −, or drag on resizing handles.

Resource library   (Vertical toolbar) Range of resources appears in bottom toolbar. Use navigation arrows for more of existing type, or different types.

Reveal   (Vertical toolbar, special tools) 2nd icon from left.

Ruler   (Vertical toolbar, special tools) 5th icon from left.

Save flipchart   (Vertical toolbar, Promethean man, Teachers toolbar) 3rd icon from left.

Shapes   (Vertical toolbar)

Snapshot   (Annotation tools) Picture can be 'photographed' from any application. Put into flipchart, or right click for Snap to clipboard.

Snapshot   (Vertical toolbar, special tools) Put picture into current page, new page, or right click for Snap to clipboard.

Sound   (Design mode) Click on object, select Object properties, select Click action, select Play sound, choose sound from library or own sound file.

Spotlight   (Vertical toolbar, special tools) 1st icon on left.

Text editor   (Vertical toolbar) Opens up text options in bottom toolbar. Can also be accessed by clicking on existing text, and selecting T icon.

Undo and redo   Vertical toolbar

Wipe clean menu   (Vertical toolbar) Three options: clear page, remove all objects, remove all scribbles.

Reference Table for SMARTboard version 8.1.2, 2004

Note Text in **bold** type: Function
Text in parentheses: Where to find the function

Attachments (View>attachments, or icon on bottom right of window) Allows other files to be attached to a notebook page.
Background colour (Format>background colour)
Clear page (Edit>select all>delete or Ctrl A, delete)
Copy (Edit>copy or Ctrl C)
Cut (Edit>cut or Ctrl X)
Editing text Double click on text.
Eraser (Floating tools) User hand or from pen tray.
Eraser (Draw>eraser) Cannot be used without board attached.
Full screen view (View>full screen) Hides toolbars.
Handwriting recognition (Select freehand text, then tap on A symbol) Can only be used with board attached.
Hyperlink (Insert>hyperlink) Text or object can be linked to webpage.
New notebook (File>new or Ctrl N)
New page (Insert>blank page or icon)
Open notebook (File>open or Ctrl O)
Page navigation (Page sorter icons on right)
Paste (Edit>paste or Ctrl V)
Pen, highlighter (Floating tools) Use finger or from pen tray.
Pen, highlighter (Draw>pen, Draw>highlighter or icon) Highlighter icon not on simple toolbar.
Pictures (Insert>clip art) Range of folders to choose from. Can also navigate to own picture files.
Print (File>print or Ctrl P)
Redo (Icon (not simple toolbar) or Ctrl Y)
Resizing objects Select, then drag on bottom right circle.
Save (File>save or Ctrl S)
Screen Capture (View>screen capture or icon) Can also be used with other applications. Choice of area, window or screen. Pictures can be saved to current page or new page.
Screen Capture (Floating tools) Can also be used with other applications. Choice of area, window or screen. Pictures can be saved to current page or new page.
Screen shade (View>screen shade or icon (not simple toolbar))
Shapes (Draw menu or icons (not on simple toolbar)) Range of shapes and lines available. Format menu for colour, width etc.
Sound/video (SMART video player) Attach sound or video file.

Spotlight (Floating tools)

Template (Insert>browse for page template) Range of folders to choose from. Can save own also.

Typed text Start typing. Use Format>text to change font, etc.

Undo (Icon or Ctrl Z)

Index